WITHDRAWN

Twayne's United States Authors Series

Sidney Howard

TUSAS 288

Sidney Howard

SIDNEY HOWARD

By SIDNEY HOWARD WHITE
University of Rhode Island

TWAYNE PUBLISHERS
A DIVISION OF G. K. HALL & CO., BOSTON

Library of Congress Cataloging in Publication Data

White, Sidney Howard.
  Sidney Howard.

  (Twayne's United States authors series; TUSAS 288)
  Bibliography: pp. 163–73
  Includes index.
  1. Howard, Sidney Coe, 1891–1939—Criticism and interpre-
tation. I. Title.
PS3515.0847Z9   812′.5′2   77–24471
ISBN 0–8057–7191–3

As always,
To Phyllis

Contents

About the Author

Preface

Acknowledgments

Chronology

1.	The Life	19
2.	The Early Work	36
3.	*They Knew What They Wanted*	49
4.	Plays of the 1920's . . . *The Silver Cord*	60
5.	Plays of the 1930's . . . *Bean* . . . *Dodsworth*	83
6.	Last Plays . . . *Yellow Jack*	105
7.	The Hollywood Years	125
8.	Evaluations	133
	Notes and References	147
	Selected Bibliography	163
	Index	175

About the Author

Sidney Howard White is Professor of English at the University of Rhode Island. A New Englander by birth, he has lived for many years in Southern California, where he completed his undergraduate work at Loyola University and graduate work (M.A., Ph.D.) at the University of Southern California. He considers the years at Loyola University probably the most influential of his life, where amidst an "alien" religious culture he was warmly welcomed and served as editor of the newspaper for four years.

From 1953 to 1966, Dr. White was Associate Professor and Head of the Department of English at Marymount College, Palos Verdes Estates, California. He has taught Creative Writing and Literature at the University of California at Los Angeles Extension, and has been Visiting Professor of English at the University of Victoria, British Columbia. He has also published stories and poems, as well as having plays produced at the Marymount theater.

Dr. White returned to the East in 1966 to be Director of English Studies in Extension for the University of Rhode Island, a post he held for five years. He now devotes himself to teaching and research, having published books on *The Scarlet Letter*, *The Great Gatsby*, and Arthur Miller. He regularly gives graduate seminars on Emerson, Hawthorne, Henry James, the 1920's, and Dramatic Literature.

Dr. White served with the U. S. Army in World War II in Okinawa in an anti-aircraft radar unit. He is also a former president of the College English Association of Southern California, and a member of the Executive Board of the California Association of Teachers of English.

Preface

For nearly twenty years during the 1920's and 1930's Sidney Howard was a major factor in the American theater. His physical presence alone—usually bristling with high energy and great vitality—was fairly well accepted as part of that marvelous matrix of New York Broadway life that makes up the Gotham legend. Howard was respected, admired by fellow playwrights, well paid both in New York and Hollywood (the highest paid screenwriter of his time)—and then suddenly in 1939 everything came to a tragic halt with a fatal tractor accident on his farm. The mere facts of these twenty years reveal not only the creative products of an alert mind, but also the 1920's and 1930's with the values, the ideals, the curious cross purposes of an exciting age. He was, as Joseph Wood Krutch has pointed out, a man of his time, concerned with the human condition but never a theorist alone—"one of the most intelligent but least intellectual; one of the most serious but least solemn . . . convinced that plays had to do with people and situations, not with what are called 'ideas.' "[1]

The critical reputation has been fairly secure; *Time* in 1934 in granting Eugene O'Neill the first place in U.S. playwriting, placed Howard close behind in company with Philip Barry and Maxwell Anderson.[2] Innovations in stagecraft, particularly with *Yellow Jack* (1934), brought a number of favorable comparisons with O'Neill. Alan Downer holds that Howard "revealed an understanding of the possibilities of the physical medium second only to that of Eugene O'Neill among his contemporaries."[3] What, of course, must be explored here are the markings and measures of a capable playwright who was more than merely suitable in his own time. Necessary questions come to mind about Howard's view of life (realistic if not tragic), of public morals (comic if not obsessed), of human love (sympathetic if not cynical)—and above all, of the artist as subject (the free spirit more than the troubled). In the matter of social justice, comparisons with Arthur Miller of the next generation are of interest. *The Ghost of Yankee Doodle* (1937) and Miller's *All My Sons* (1947) provide two views of family moral conscience tested by improper munitions sales during wartime.

I have at all times in this inquiry been fascinated with the person of Howard, the impressive movement of this man from coast to coast on various writing tasks, the prodigious accomplishments in numbers alone—twenty-seven plays produced in New York, thirteen or more film scripts, seven short stories, numerous pieces of socially aware journalism. His career as a volunteer ambulance driver and pilot in World War I, intent, as he was, on being part of a great experience "before it was all gone," mark him engagingly as a young American to be admired. In letters home to his mother during these years he reveals an almost old-fashioned notion of family duty, a concern about what must be done in the name of *all* the Howards: "You call it unhealthy thirst for excitement. Unhealthy, oh my dear— when there is so much to do and one is twenty-five and going to be young only a *little* time longer! And the place to be young is the dangerous place."[4] It is this kind of enthusiasm that characterizes Howard's writing, characterizes the faults as well as the virtues. At times, according to Glenn Hughes, the headstrong way was "apt to carry him beyond the bounds of dramatic propriety."[5] The reference here may well be to the numerous strong-willed heroines who have become Howard trade marks.

Certainly, no heroine was more engagingly controversial than Amy in the Pulitzer Prize winning *They Knew What They Wanted* (1924). Pragmatist to the core, she faces up to contemporary morality and will make the best of what could be called a faultless seduction. Other heroines, such as Elsa in *Alien Corn* (1933), or Carrie in *Ned McCobb's Daughter* (1926) do, however, test our credulity somewhat in the forceful ways they solve their problems. Howard's own exuberance, never even thinly disguised, animates such characters. They seem, at times, to be doing no more than reacting powerfully and emotionally to strong stimuli. Here, of course, is the basis of the charge that Howard writes melodramatically and lacks the subtlety of complex characterizations. Nevertheless, as Walter Meserve points out, in his history of social dramas in the 1920's, Howard does seem to have an "epoch-marking sense of humanity" and excellent "insights into social morality."[6]

Our inquiry, therefore, is into the plays and into the life of the energetic young man of the 1920's and the 1930's who never seemed to disavow the direct assaults against smallness in life; or, for that matter, to condone pettiness when nobility seemed in order, or timidity when overriding courage was called for. He peopled his dramatic world with a wide variety of what might be called old-fashioned champions of liberty and freedom. I am also concerned about attitudes as well as accomplishments. Sidney Howard held decided views on dramaturgy, notably the conviction (possibly from his actress wife Clare Eames) that playwriting existed primarily for the actor, that the dramatist was actually a "vicarious actor." Further questions to be considered include Howard's long list of adaptations and translations and what his involvement with them meant to his career. (Hughes, for one, holds that they were a continual diversion from original work.)

The approach in this study will be chronological and selective. Naturally, in nearly twenty years of writing, some portions of the twenty-seven plays and thirteen screenplays carry far greater weight than others. Our interest in Howard is primarily as a playwright; the screenplays are reviewed in one chapter, in which the interest, at times, is as much biographical as critical. Howard's encounter with Hollywood, particularly in the making of *Gone With the Wind* (1939), is a fascinating record of the essential playwright wrestling with a different art form in a somewhat "alien country." The concentration, therefore, will be on thirteen major plays which show his development as a force in American theater. The basis for selections allows such box office failures as *Lucky Sam McCarver* (1925), *Half Gods* (1929), and *Paths of Glory* (1935)—contributions, nevertheless, to our critical understanding.

Attention, of course, will be centered on *They Knew What They Wanted*, which, to many, brought sex to Broadway for the first time, charming and winsome though the essential story may be. Other successes will include *Ned McCobb's Daughter*, which together with *Lucky Sam McCarver* introduced the gangster world to Broadway; *The Silver Cord* (1926), a study of momism; and *The Late Christopher Bean* (1932), a popular favorite revealing Howard's singular ability as an adapter. Most critics would probably agree that the 1934 dramatization of Sinclair Lewis' novel, *Dodsworth*, was the high-water mark among Howard's many translations and adaptations. The fact that Howard was to be involved with fourteen such tasks for the theater probably explains to some extent his equal ability in transferring other men's works into screenplays.

Two other literary activities concern us: the journalism and the short stories. The years as a somewhat crusading radical journalist (1920–1924) will be treated in Chapter One. Evaluations of the seven short stories, also primarily products of the early 1920's, will appear in Chapter Two, together with appraisals of a few early plays. The final chapter, Evaluations, will attempt to draw together a number of assessments-along-the-way into some unified major views of Howard's total accomplishments. Among these, notably, will be his views on modern women, modern morality, and the writers' craft. Our involvement with such an engaging personality as Howard should be a delight as well as an instructive pleasure; and I believe we will find the truth of this as we watch the plays speak for themselves of the essential robustness of an intriguing man of his age.

SIDNEY HOWARD WHITE

University of Rhode Island

Acknowledgments

To the Director of the Bancroft Library, University of California, Berkeley, for permission to quote from the Sidney Coe Howard Collection.

To Walter D. Howard to quote from the Howard Collection, Berkeley.

To the New York *Times* for permission to quote from articles and reviews which appeared as follows:

Sidney Howard, "Sidney Howard Speaking," March 20, 1927.

Mordaunt Hall, "Condemned," November 4, 1929.

Sidney Howard, "Views of the Motion Picture Industry," December 1, 1929.

Mordaunt Hall, "Arrowsmith," December 8, 1931.

Sidney Howard, "G.P.B. of Harvard and Yale," February 5, 1933.

Brooks Atkinson, "Alien Corn," February 21, 1933.

Frank Nugent, "Dodsworth," September 24, 1936.

Sidney Howard, "Waking, Not Walking, the Ghost," November 21, 1937.

Frank Nugent, "GWTW," December 20, 1939.

Brooks Atkinson, "Madame, Will You Walk?," December 2, 1953.

To *Commonweal* for permission to quote from the review by Richard Dana Skinner which appeared March 15, 1933.

To *The Nation* for permission to quote from reviews which appeared as follows:

Ludwig Lewisohn, "Drama: Homespun and Brocade," September 21, 1921.

Joseph Wood Krutch, "Ned McCobb's Daughter," December 29, 1926.

————, "Drama: A Peevish Play," January 8, 1930.

————, "Alien Corn," March 15, 1933.

————, "The Silver Cord," September 13, 1933.

————, "Yellow Jack," March 21, 1934.

Harold Clurman, "Madame, Will You Walk?," December 19, 1953.

To *The New Republic* for permission to quote from a review which appeared February 9, 1927; and from Sidney Howard, "Hollywood on the Slide," November 9, 1932.

To *Modern Drama* for permission to quote from the article by Walter J. Meserve, "Sidney Howard and the Social Drama of the Twenties," December, 1963.

To W. W. Norton for permission to quote from John Mason Brown, *Upstage*, 1930.

To Charles Scribner's Sons for permission to quote from Sidney Howard, "Preface," *Lucky Sam McCarver*, 1926; and Sidney Howard, "Such Women as Ellen Steele," *Scribner's Magazine*, January, 1925.

To Kennikat Press for permission to quote from Barrett Clark, *Intimate Portraits*, 1970.

To the New York *Daily News* for permission to quote from the review by John Chapman, "Lute Song," February 7, 1946.

To the New York *Post* for permission to quote from the following:
Michael Mok, "Sidney Howard Loves Nearly Everything Except Things Like Social Messages," August 16, 1939.
Richard Watts, Jr., "Madame, Will You Walk?" December 15, 1953.

Chronology

1891   June 26—Sidney Coe Howard born in Oakland, California, to John Lawrence Howard and Helen Louise Coe Howard. Father, steamship executive; large, musically inclined family.

1903   First extended trip to Europe.

1910   TB sanatorium, Switzerland, for a year.

1911   University of California at Berkeley, where he majored in English and classical literature, and wrote for school publications.

1914   First play, *The Sons of Spain*, produced as pageant for artist's colony at Carmel.

1915   Graduation from Berkeley. High grades. Enrolls at Harvard in Baker's English 47. Active university and theater life, writing and attending plays.

1916   Leaves for European war: two and a half years as ambulance driver in France and Balkans, and later as pilot for French and U.S. forces.

1919   Begins journalism career with *Life*.

1920   "The Stars in Their Courses," *Collier's* short story, first publication.

1920   Socially conscious reporter for Hearst and others for four years. Articles on Communist witch-hunts, super patriots, stock and oil swindles, and labor union infiltrations. Reputation as radical reporter and liberal.

1921   September 1—*Swords* opened in New York for 36 performances. Failure.

1922   January 2—S.S. *Tenacity* opened in New York for 67 performances. This translation from Charles Vildrac was to be the first of many translations and adaptations of limited success.

1922   Marries Clare Eames, actress.

1923 European travel: journalism assignments, active play-writing.

1924 October 1—*Bewitched* (written with Edward Sheldon) opened in New York for 29 performances.

1924 *Three Flights Up*, short story collection, published.

1924 November 24—*They Knew What They Wanted* opened in New York for 414 performances; awarded *Pulitzer Prize*, great success. Fights censorship battles and wins; becomes spokesman for the theater.

1925 Pageant *Lexington* presented at Lexington, Massachusetts.

1925 October 21—*Lucky Sam McCarver* opened in New York for 29 performances. A bitter failure.

1926 Clare Eames elected to Board of Managers of the Theatre Guild.

1926 November 29—*Ned McCobb's Daughter* opened in New York for 132 performances.

1926 December 20—*The Silver Cord* opened in New York for 112 performances.

1928 Separation from Clare. "At home" at sister's house in Berkeley for next two years. Despondent.

1929 Hollywood career as screen writer begins. Contract with Samuel Goldwyn.

1929 "The Homesick Ladies," *Scribner's Magazine*, wins Second Prize in annual O. Henry short story competition.

1929 December 21—*Half Gods* opened in New York for 17 performances. Great disappointment.

1930 March—Divorce from Clare. November—death of Clare in London nursing home.

1930 September 1—*Lute Song*, presented in Stockbridge; initial New York production (elaborate), 1946.

1931 *Arrowsmith* screenplay wins Academy Award.

1931 Marries Leopoldine Blaine Damrosch.

1932 October 31—*The Late Christopher Bean* opened in New York for 224 performances. The most successful adaptation.

1933 February 20—*Alien Corn* opened in New York for 96 per-formances. Major personal success for Katherine Cornell.

1934 February 24—*Dodsworth* opened in New York for 278 performances, financially the most rewarding. The screen-play in 1936 was much admired.

Chronology

1934   March 6—*Yellow Jack* opened in New York for 79 performances. Innovative staging.

1934   November 10—Honorary degree, Washington and Jefferson College.

1935   Elected President, Dramatists Guild of the Author's League of America; two years actively in office.

1935   September 26—*Paths of Glory* opened in New York for 23 performances.

1935   Bought five hundred-acre dairy farm in Tyringham, Massachusetts, where he began to spend much time actively involved with prize herds, plowing, gardening.

1936   Signed by David O. Selznick to do screenplay of *Gone With the Wind*; posthumously awarded Academy Award for best script of 1939.

1937   October 28—*The Ghost of Yankee Doodle* opened in New York for 48 performances.

1938   Joins in formation of Playwrights' Producing Co. with Robert Sherwood, Elmer Rice, S. N. Behrman, Maxwell Anderson, and lawyer, John F. Wharton.

1939   August 23—death by tractor accident at Tyringham farm.

1953   December 1—*Madam, Will You Walk?* opened in New York for 42 performances, the last Howard production.

CHAPTER 1

The Life

SIDNEY Howard was born June 26, 1891, in Oakland, California, the son of John Lawrence Howard, steamship executive ("capitalist" he wrote on Howard's birth certificate) and Helen Louise Coe, professional organist and piano teacher. Serious music seemed to be a family tradition. The father directed singing societies in Philadelphia and in California, and was described by Howard as a veritable "Handel hound," who had his large family "learn Handel choruses as kids and keep time."[1] The fact that both his parents were of pioneer stock seemed a matter of importance to Howard. Even further, the parts played by his grandfather and father in opening Oregon, Washington, and Alaska to ship traffic probably provided the basis for his keen sense of national pride and personal responsibility. Continual references to the "Howard name" are not romantic gesturings alone; they were very real and tangible demonstrations of his essential American spirit. No other characteristic is so often indicated by those who knew him best.

The young Howard was an earnest member of a comfortable, active, close knit family. "I went to public schools," he writes to Barrett Clark, "and read books and camped in the high Sierras and rode horses and went to British Columbia and Mexico" (Clark, p. 211). In general, however, his health was not good; tuberculosis in his early teens sent him to a ranch in Ojai Valley (near Los Angeles) and eventually to a Swiss sanitarium at the age of nineteen in 1910. Early diaries and picture journals reveal that he was a careful traveller, meticulous in the collection and posting of what could be called "documents of the trip," whether in British Columbia or eventually in Europe. The first-hand knowledge of Europe began early: In 1903 and 1904 at the age of twelve he lived in Europe for six months with his mother and half-sister Jean. Early signs of the avid museum-

19

goer and sincere appreciator of art fill the charming and perceptive letters to his father. He seems well prepared in his views;
Andrea Del Sarto, for example, is a favorite painter whom he can
write about with youthful zeal—and knowledge.

I *The University*

In 1911, a few years older than the average freshman (due
to his illness), Howard entered the University of California at
Berkeley. His father's illness prevented the first choice, Harvard.
The college career is one of industry and involvement. He re-
ceived high grades, gave the final convocation for the Senior
Class, wrote for the campus periodicals, became editor of *The
Occident*, the literary periodical, in his sophomore year. He even
tried a little acting in college productions. A major interest in
writing (poetry, short stories, essays) was quickly developing.
Drama in time became the focus of his attention. His first play,
The Sons of Spain, was written for Professor Leonard Bacon's
Poetry Seminar. Originally conceived as a medieval piece, it was
later changed to an early California setting for the artists' colony
at Carmel where it was produced as a pageant in 1914. Other
productions at the university included the Junior Farce and the
Senior Class pageant. In 1915 at the age of twenty-four he
graduated with excellent grades, having majored in English.

Despite the prominence of George Pierce Baker and his theater
work at Harvard, it was actually Harvard itself that really drew
Howard the following September.[2] However, in time the influence
of Harvard on him was to be synonymous with the word, Baker.
"He taught his students truth" as more valid than technique,
Howard reported many years later. Art, according to Baker, was
an obligation, a professional task.[3] The theatrical and intellectual
environment was a heady one for the young Californian. His
classmates in English 47 included S. N. Behrman, Lewis Beach,
and Edward Massey. Letters home to his mother ("I read and
think about the world") are brimfull with the new, exciting
Cambridge life.[4] During the year he wrote a variety of plays
for Baker: a modern mystery play, adaptations from the works
of John Galsworthy and Rudyard Kipling. He also read the
sixteenth and seventeenth century playwrights (Ben Jonson,

Beaumont and Fletcher) and wrote his master's thesis on John Lyly's plays. He soon became an active theater-goer in Boston and New York. He was determined to be a playwright; he was teeming with ideas ranging from "a powerful birth control play" to Jane Austen high comedy. The complete role of the artist, he wrote his mother, was what he wanted for himself; to be actively involved in life (not in scholarship): "Give me the guy who stakes his life on his ambitions and sees them through anything."[5]

II *The War*

By the spring of 1916, with the European war almost into its third year, Howard along with so many other young men was becoming restless with the role of bystander. A theatrical involvement at this time was probably the only thing that kept him momentarily away from Europe. Under the influence of Samuel Hume of Harvard, Howard wrote "The Cranbrook Masque," an outdoor pageant for private production in Michigan. And then, in July as Howard himself reports, he "took the first liner" to France to join the volunteer ambulance corps.

Howard's two and a half years in the military, from the age of twenty-five to twenty-eight—certainly not a callow youth—were to have a marked effect on his entire life. The firsthand experiences at the French (and the Balkan) front as an ambulance driver, and later as a combat pilot, provided a storehouse of impressions. He was marked for life, one might say, as the sensitive young man who had seen too much of social devastation and military ineptness. It was the making of a realist in the theater. There was the additional factor of his own country's hesitation in joining a just conflict. It was clear-cut to him why the war had to be fought—and won. Civilization was in the balance. Individual moral character was involved. He wrote to his mother on October 21, 1916: "The great thing about this job is the mere fact of being always ready for what may come and seeing anything through. That is good for a man. It is good for a man to find out how little his physical discomfort can be allowed to matter to a real job—to be always at the order of a man behind a stove and to have to go out and freeze for two hours for some poor hound and not for himself."[6]

He was, of course, continually gathering "writers' impressions"; he urged his mother to keep all his letters since they were his working journal. His first published short story, "The Stars in Their Courses" (1920), was to describe a comrade in Albania who acts heroically to save a little Moslem girl.[7] He read widely in foreign literatures—Brunetiere, Machiavelli, Spinoza, Voltaire, Balzac, Emile Zola—and evidently sharpened his already excellent knowledge of languages. This ability was to be evident in the fourteen translations and adaptations he was to do for the stage.[8]

In time he became a combat pilot for the French, and after the United States entry into the war, a lieutenant in the Air Service. His feelings about aviation were widely shared by many others of his generation. Fliers were the romantic, lone heroes of the war, knights of the air compared to the anonymous soldiers in the trenches. "It's sport," he wrote home to his sister, "and by God, it's poetry."[9] This is not to say, of course, that he took the war lightly; it merely reaffirms the basic romantic heroism of the man. He was also able to distinguish, at the same time, the difference in his new comrades. Compared to the French and Albanian soldiers whom he had lived with for over a year, the Americans were like college sophomores. His own record, by the time his service ended in January, 1919, was characteristic: he was twice cited for gallantry in action and was awarded the Silver Star.[10]

III   *Journalist*

Out of uniform and a more than mature twenty-eight, Sidney Howard set out in 1919 to resume the pursuit of letters in New York City. The first actual job was with the old *Life,* then a weekly humor magazine. By 1922 he had advanced from reading eight hundred jokes a day to the position of Literary Editor. He also maintained his connections with Samuel Hume, for whom he wrote a translation of Gabrielle d'Annunzio's *Fedra.* Written for the Polish actress, Alla Nazimova, it never was produced in New York.[11]

In late spring, 1919, Howard began the long friendship with Barrett Clark. Together they wrote an adaptation of James Branch Cabell's *The Rivet in Grandfather's Neck,* which, although failing in production, succeeded admirably in making a lasting friendship. The directness and vigor of Howard was immediately apparent to Clark: "In twenty-four hours we had started writing a play together; in another twenty-four we had begun fighting against the suppression of *Jurgen,* and in intervals, at his apartment, we were arguing out the merits of Ancient Persian music, modern German painting and American beer. The writing of the play, incidentally, proved to me that he was a playwright, and I was not" (Clark, p. 183).

It was at this time (1920–1924) that Howard began to make a name for himself as a socially conscious reporter for *Colliers, The New Republic,* and particularly, *Hearst's International.* Considering the subjects (Communist witch-hunts, labor unions, dope running, stock swindles, and oil crooks) it was, of course, sensational journalism as well. And in view of his defense of unpopular positions he was broadly labeled a radical reporter. The first of his articles, "Baiting The Bolshevist," appeared January 10, 1920 in *Colliers.* Howard's intention was to present an objective view of Russian political life in America and to urge a "square deal" for the many Russian immigrants who were undeniably loyal citizens. Citing government statistics, he pointed to the five thousand or less Bolshevists among the six hundred thousand Russian aliens in the country. The tendency during these turbulent post-war times was to blame all violence on international Communism, real or imagined.

A series of three articles followed in the spring and summer on the William Colyer trial and Judge John Anderson's unpopular decision.[12] The issue in trial was the right of the U.S. government to deport aliens who advocated the violent overthrow of the government. Anderson had ruled that the government had not followed due process, a view that Howard agreed with. The following year he was hired by an independent research bureau to do a major series of articles on the widespread business practice of infiltrating and subverting labor unions. The assignment, a collaboration with Robert Dunn, resulted in seven articles in *The New Republic,* and the articles were eventually published in book form in 1924 as *The Labor Spy.*[13] The entire project reveals a number of characteristic traits of Howard the journalist and dramatist. Immediately apparent is the direct, surprisingly individual tone in which we seem to sense the reporter's personal encounter with evil. At times, he seems to be nearly melodramatic in approach, moving swiftly from one reported improper act to another; and, at all times, he gives the scrupulous documentation at length, so that the record of the infamy can speak for itself. "No matter how realistic an article," he later confided to Clark, "or how faithful its reporting, it requires an emotional objective and direction" (Clark, p. 199). The results were usually something beyond the routine obligations of a journalistic assignment.

The series was admired by the Hearst Publications and it secured for Howard additional assignments in America and Europe. During 1923, under Norman Hapgood's guidance, nearly an article a month appeared in the Hearst papers.[14] The subjects included oil and stock swindles and the narcotics market. The style of writing was in the Hearst manner of personal interviews, abundant dialogue, and many examples—and all heavily illustrated. During 1924 Howard continued in this vein with a series of five articles in *The New Republic* on the topic of over zealous patriotism.[15] In the same objective manner as *The Labor Spy,* he exposed the organized attempts in the country to subvert free speech and thought under the guise of postwar patriotism. The inquiry ultimately came under the wing of Hapgood in a publication he edited in 1927, titled *Professional Patriots* with material assembled by Howard and John Hearley. The title page carries the following legend: "An Exposure of the Personalities, Methods, and Objectives Involved in the Organized Effort to Exploit Patriotic Impulses in These United States During and after the Late War."[16]

The book is a good model for works of this kind, designed to provide a kind of ready handbook to the average citizen on dangers to his liberties. Opening with impressive endorsements by contemporary leaders (William Allen White, Congressman La-Guardia, Professor Felix Frankfurter, etc.) it presents a well organized collection of facts and figures on organizations such as the National Civic Federation, National Security League, American Defense Society, and even the American Legion. The contention seems well documented that civil liberties are seriously endangered. Editor Hapgood's "call to arms" obviously has

Howard in the front ranks: "The liberals," he urges, "if they do their job, should be busy also."[17] Such journalistic commitments were to show themselves best in the late (1937) play, *The Ghost of Yankee Doodle.*

IV *Stage Novice*

Howard's thirtieth year (1921) was a busy and eventful one: travels to Europe for Hearst, numerous translations, adaptations,[18] and original plays in preparation; the first production on Broadway; and—at the end of the year—his engagement to Clare Eames the actress. The first production was the poetic drama, *Swords,* September 1, 1921, which despite its failure received praise for imaginative writing and, particularly, Robert Edmond Jones' romantic set.[19] It was a beginning for the young playwright, painful as the experience was. Barrett Clark tells of the evening in the company of George Pierce Baker: "After the final curtain, G.P.B. looked into Howard's tear-brimming eyes and began to chuckle, and the tears turned to laughter and they both laughed until they cried, and Howard never wrote again in verse."[20]

At least one fortunate result of *Swords* was the meeting with Clare Jennes Eames, who was cast in the lead. Born in Cleveland and trained in Paris, Clare made her Broadway debut in 1918 in *The Big Scene.* In the 1920–21 season she starred as Mary Stuart in the John Drinkwater play. Laurence Langer described her as "tall, distinguished, and vibrant" with a "sheer joy of living."[21] Her regal appearance had her appearing in various plays as Queen Elizabeth and Mary of Scotland. In 1923 she was called to Hollywood by Mary Pickford to appear with her as Queen Elizabeth in the film, *Dorothy Vernon of Haddon Hall.* The failure of *Swords,* as Howard good humorously told a friend, was in a way secondary; "the real purpose of this play was to marry us."[22] Which he did on June 1, 1922.

Howard's second Broadway venture, *S.S. Tenacity* (1922), was produced in New York at the beginning of the year and had a fair amount of success with sixty-seven performances. Charles Vildrac, the author of the original, was widely acclaimed in France and beyond for a refreshingly new truth and sincerity in theater.[23] Howard was greatly influenced by the original, admitting it changed him from the romantic and theatrical to the realistic and uncontrived. Nevertheless, in the last half of 1922 he collaborated with Edward Sheldon to write *Bewitched*, "a Freudian Fairy Tale," as he called it. It was produced in 1924. It did not do well: most critics agreed with Robert Littell ("Hash, poetry, and philosophy poured slowly like rather thick cream");[24] and only a few with Stephen Vincent Benet who admired the magic.[25] The year, as all years now, was increasingly busy, his time divided between journalism for Hearst, his position at *Life*, and more plays. He had plans, he wrote to Clark, for three more: one on a California ranch, a modern comedy, and one on St. Francis. He summed up his new life as "being married and gloriously happy and ingloriously broke" (Clark, p. 193).

The greater part of 1923 was spent in Europe. From this time we have a rather amusing picture of Howard and his wife seeking whatever privacy they can find while being "pursued" by his widowed mother and her motor car in Europe. July in Venice saw the beginning of the first draft of *They Knew What They Wanted*; August included a trip to Prague to do a memoir of President Masaryk for Hearst. (Nothing came of this since Masaryk had recently completed his own.) While in Italy, Howard heard the reports of the failure of *Casanova* which opened in New York September 26. Sailing home in October on the *Scythia*, their vessel collided with the *Cedric* in the fog. Howard reported that in the panic of a possible abandonment of the ship he grabbed the two things that he valued most: the manuscript of *They Knew What They Wanted* and a statuette of Shakespeare. Fortunately, desperate measures were not needed and they merely returned to port and took another vessel for New York.

Additional work during the winter in California on *They Knew What They Wanted* was followed by another opening in New York, *Sancho Panza*, on November 26. Another failure. (It should be noted that despite the meager acceptance of the many adaptations and translations througout his career, there continued a steady demand on Broadway to make the attempts. The original plays were usually outstanding successes in Europe and evidently it was worth while to "do something" with them for the American audience.) Howard and his wife continued in their active New York life: Clare going on from one success on Broadway to another, even including occasional films on Long Island and California; Howard, dividing his time between journalism and the plays. The highpoint of the year came in November with the publication of a book of short stories[26] and the production of *They Knew What They Wanted.*

V They Knew What They Wanted

Howard's most famous play did not find a ready acceptance; sixteen managers turned it down before the Theatre Guild accepted it. Many factors were against it, including the unfamiliar setting and the many dialects. Nevertheless, it became the outstanding play of 1924, ran for over a year, toured the country, and was produced in London the following year. The play was awarded the Pulitzer Prize, winning over *What Price Glory* and *Desire Under the Elms.* Among other things it brought his journalism career to a halt. He had been hired by the New York *World* to begin the day after the opening of the play. Editor Bayard Swope read the review of his drama critic, Heywood Broun, and telephoned Howard in his bed, "I see by the morning papers you don't need a job, you're fired."[27]

Among the changes that this success brought to his life was the beginning of his major role as spokesman for the theater. In many ways he was a natural to play this part. With his keen directness and relentless honesty he had earlier been singled out by Clark and others as a man to center on. The censorship attacks against *They Knew What They Wanted* and *Desire Under the Elms* because of adulteries, pregnancies, and child murder brought the issues of theatrical freedom out into the open. In 1925 the city fathers in New York began a "clean-play" crusade. They formed Play Juries drawn from a cross section of playgoers. Their "examination" of *They Knew* and *Desire* resulted in an acquittal; nevertheless, the Will Hays Office soon after banned *They Knew* from the films.[28] Two years later, with increasing controversy building in New York and Los Angeles, New York District Attorney Banton decided to go beyond the Play Juries and to prosecute where necessary. At this time the theater appointed

a committee of their own to regulate themselves, which included
Winthrop Ames, Frank Gillmore, and Sidney Howard.

Church pressure in Albany brought about the introduction of
the Jenkes Bill in the Assembly, which would establish a
Division of Dramatics to read all plays before New York production. The committee hearings provided the first public forum
for Howard to speak out for the theater. Representing the Author's League and the Association of American Dramatists, Howard pointed out the fallibility of punishing playwrights before
the fact; he argued for the continuance of the Play Juries which
at least gave opinions after the fact. The fight was eventually
won and the bill defeated.[29]

Although Howard had to wait until 1926 to repeat the success of *They Knew* of 1924, he was far from idle in the interval.
The year 1925 saw the largest number of Howard plays on
Broadway; four openings (and four failures), which included
one original and three translations.[30] In addition, the pageant,
Lexington, which he wrote for the one hundred and fiftieth anniversary of the Republic, was performed during the week of
June 16, 1925 at Lexington. The failure of *Lucky Sam McCarver,*
the one original, was difficult to accept considering the very high
hopes he had for it. Howard thought it his best play, and a few
critics agreed despite the general lack of interest.[31] Not to be
outdone, he also began a collaboration with Will Irwin during
the year, the adaptation of the ancient Chinese classic *Pi-Pa-Ki*
into the musical *Lute Song.* However, the play remained unsold,
and aside from a 1930 production in Stockbridge, did not see
Broadway until the posthumous production of 1946.

The two successes of 1926 were *Ned McCobb's Daughter* and
The Silver Cord. The plays were well suited to the contemporary
taste, the strong interest in assertive women who in Henry James'
phrase, "confronted their destiny." The plays were listed on
nearly everyone's ten best plays of the season. Clare played the
lead in *Ned McCobb's Daughter* and later starred in the London
production of *The Silver Cord.* Her health remained a critical
issue during these years although she was able to serve on the
Board of Managers of the Theatre Guild. At home they divided
their time between New York City and a rented farm in Wiscasset, Maine, which Howard once described as a "Victorian

palace" of superlative comfort. However, the various separations
(particularly in London) began to have their toll on the marriage; by 1928 Howard was confiding to his mother that he
couldn't understand the strange "London bunch" she was with.
Clare returned from London in March and promptly sailed again
in May. The formal separation had begun.

VI   *Enter Hollywood*

For the next few years (1928–29), if the distraught playwright
was to be home anywhere, it was in Berkeley, California, at the
home of his half-sister Jean—Mrs. Duncan McDuffie. He was
comforted to some extent by his financially rewarding entrance
into screen writing. With the assurance of Samuel Goldwyn that
he would make him a millionaire, he signed to write for the new
star, Ronald Colman. A number of scripts followed including
Bull Dog Drummond, Condemned, and *Raffles* for Colman.
During the next ten years Howard was to write over a dozen
scripts as well as revisions and partial work on at least seven
more by other writers. In short order his craftsmanship became
widely recognized; he was valued as a construction expert,
planning the basic steps and scenes. Others, if necessary, could
do the dialogue.[32]

Another award came in April 1929 with the winning of Second
Prize in the annual O. Henry short story competition. First
planned as a play, "The Homesick Ladies" was a strange ghostlike
story of the reunion of two sisters after thirty years.[33] The contributions to the New York Stage continued without a success
(until 1932): five more plays, three of which were translations.[34] The greatest disappointment was *Half Gods,* an obvious
autobiographic rendering of his marital difficulties. He admitted
to Clark in 1930 that he was having difficulties writing himself
out of his personal doldrums: "Clare held me hard to the theater,
of course. I don't at all know what will happen to me now that
Clare's let go ... my heart seems to have gone out of that kind
of writing [plays] and hasn't yet got fixed in any other kind. I
am marking time for the moment, not liking it but being well
paid and so not complaining. I always need someone with a
club, and at the moment there isn't anyone" (Clark, p. 212).

The divorce was granted in March, 1930. With Clare still in London and the custody of their little girl, Jennifer, given to him, Howard felt the great responsibility of her upbringing. It is of interest that in the letters written to his family at this time he was insistent on his need to maintain a stolid righteousness in the entire ugly business; the welfare of his daughter was to be the first and only consideration. Unfortunately (or fortunately) the entire story of Clare in London was never to be fully known since she died the following November in a London nursing home. She had been ill for many weeks and had undergone two operations. She was buried in Richmond Cemetery outside of London.

Numerous ideas and play projects filled his mind in the early 1930's. Despite his admission in his diary that "I tire more easily and write less easily," his mind was as fertile as ever.[35] Possible subjects included the following: "Wilson and the Peace Conference, an epic drama about the revolt of the Iowa farmers against the banks, a period comedy laid in the Deep South to be adapted from a play by the Quinteros, a radical pro-labor serious play kidding the political extremists.[36] A great deal of planning went into the Wilson play, which had been in his mind since 1921; much was written and discussed with Clark and others. "The ironic tragedy of the man himself," he wrote in his diary, "too small for his great vision and too weak to command reliable support. It is a tragedy of betrayal and a comedy of idealism at the same time."[37]

Early in 1931 Howard married for the second time. He chose the socially prominent Leopoldine ("Polly") Blaine Damrosch of New York City, daughter of Walter Damrosch the conductor, and granddaughter of James G. Blaine, the U.S. statesman. Three children resulted from this union: Sidney (a daughter) 1933, Walter, 1935, and Margaret, 1938. The previous pattern of plays, films, and European travel was now extended to include a very active domestic life which ultimately resulted in the purchase of a large working farm in Tyringham, Massachusetts in 1935. The film work continued with his adaptation of Sinclair Lewis' *Arrowsmith*, which won the Academy Award in 1931 for the best screenplay. Hollywood was always a dilemma to him: neither to be resisted nor wholly accepted—Howard not being the first of many stage writers to be so affected. He confessed that the factory pressure had prevented him from seeing what he could do "beyond developing a certain technical ingenuity."[38]

VII *Theater Spokesman*

From the beginning of his prominence, he had always been concerned about young playwrights. Clark continually sent him manuscripts from promising unknowns and kept him informed. It was characteristic of Howard, according to Clark, to take direct, positive action: "The moment he read or saw a promising play he would inevitably ask him something like this: 'Has the boy got a job?—I want to see him.—He's got real talent. Would he go to the Coast for a while?' And action followed" (Clark, p. 213). Considering his well known generosity in New York and Hollywood, it was not surprising that the Playwrights' Company, following his death, established the "Sidney Howard Memorial Award" for the best first Broadway play.[39] His personal contribution in time and energy to his fellow writers reached its zenith in 1935 when he was elected President of the Dramatist Guild of the Author's League of America for a two-year term. It was a critical period for the Guild and it took a large part of his time to formulate a new Basic Agreement between authors and theatrical producers. Playwrights were being taken advantage of by the burgeoning film industry and the codification of a new set of policies was needed. Howard seemed well suited to the difficult task.[40]

The long drought of successes on Broadway ended in 1932 with the resounding success of *The Late Christopher Bean,* which ran for 224 performances. The story of the comic battles over the famous paintings of a penniless, deceased artist was derived from a play by René Fauchois. It is the one adaptation or translation—at least at the box office—which turned out to be more than hackwork. Another fair success, *Alien Corn,* followed in 1933. Katherine Cornell was so taken with the part of a music teacher "under wraps" in a women's college that she bought the part for herself and produced it. However, most of 1933 was spent working with Sinclair Lewis on his *Dodsworth.*

The eventual production of the play on February 24, 1934 marked the high-water mark of Howard's reputation. Financially, it was the most successful of all his plays, ran for a year and a half on Broadway, toured the country, and appeared in London in 1938. Lewis, not an easy man to work with, had admired Howard's *Arrowsmith* scenario and was certain he was the only playwright who could do justice to his best-selling novel. The "collaboration" involved long sessions in New York City and Lewis' Vermont farm; the result was an entirely "new creation," as Arthur Quinn described it.[41] Lewis' admiration was such that he agreed with Howard to include a lengthy account of the process of dramatization in the published volume. Not everything that Howard did with Lewis, however, turned out successfully. A scenario of *It Can't Happen Here* was abandoned by MGM due to Hays Office pressure in 1936. It was forbidden to say "Fascist" but allowed to say, "Democracy is no good."[42]

Since 1931, Howard had had the play *Yellow Jack* in mind; finally on March 6, 1934, it opened in New York. The story about the conquest of Yellow Fever by Walter Reed in Cuba was a difficult and new challenge to Howard. It involved new techniques in stage craft which were generally admired—admired enough to make it an "esteemed failure." Nevertheless, the play has become one of the most popular in the non-professional theater. The year that started out so well with the February production of *Dodsworth* still ended well with the awarding of an honorary degree by Washingon and Jefferson College in November, 1934.

After 1934, until his death in 1939, there were no more major successes on Broadway. Nevertheless, three stand out among a number of attempts as significant enterprises. *Paths of Glory* of 1935 was a much admired adaptation of the Humphrey Cobb novel. It involved the controversial issues of military blunders in high places. Still controversial, it was made into a remarkable film in 1957 by Stanley Kubrick. Even more energy went into *The Ghost of Yankee Doodle* (1937), Howard's ambitious attempt to delineate warmongers and peace advocates. It was remarkably prophetic for 1937, set as it was "eighteen months after the start of the next world war." The last play, *Madam, Will You Walk?*, was an entirely new departure for Howard, an ethical fantasy set in Central Park. It had been scheduled in 1939 to be a production of the new Playwrights' Company, with Howard directing. It was not produced in New York until 1953.

The Playwrights' Company, an undeniable milestone in Broadway theater history, began in April 1938. Spearheaded by Robert Sherwood, it was designed to combat the ills of commercial production by having five noted playwrights produce their own plays.[43] Notwithstanding its high accomplishments, the Theatre Guild *was* the adversary, particularly to Sherwood, Elmer Rice, and Maxwell Anderson. Although less disenchanted with the Guild, Howard needed little urging to join in the general dissatisfaction with New York producers. The chance to control their own wares was a daring challenge. More persuasion, however, was needed to convince S. N. Behrman that they should strike out on their own. Behrman felt indebted to the Guild for a number of major productions; and, further, had no real desire to produce other men's plays. Pursuing his own royalties was the only battle he really wanted. However, as he recorded later, he was no match for the affable and charming Sherwood, and soon joined.[44] There was no denying the basic attraction of being in association with playwrights of such noted accomplishment and individual appeal.

For Howard, the demands of the association meant long and full involvements with the productions of his colleagues. Evidently, he took to these tasks with great enthusiasm; Behrman and the others were soon to note how right Howard's judgments usually were. Much of the success of the first year's productions—Sherwood's *Abe Lincoln in Illinois,* which won a Pulitzer Prize, and Anderson's *Knickerbocker Holiday*—was due to Howard's early attention and concerns.

VIII   Gone With the Wind

One major accomplishment remained for Howard in these last few years—and it was not in the New York theater. Ironically it was Hollywood, ambivalent master and mistress to so many writing talents, which provided the crowning accomplishment to his career. The film, *GWTW,* which he wrote but never saw, earned him another Academy Award in 1939. From the very start of the project in 1936, Howard had been David O. Selznick's first choice for the difficult task of reducing Margaret Mitchell's thousand-page novel into a film. Despite differences during the long drawn-out preparations, Selznick never really altered his respect for the playwright. Even as late as September 1938, he could refer to Howard in a letter to Ed Sullivan as "one of America's distinguished playwrights . . . one of the best scenarists in the world."[45] The one basic problem—which Selznick was forced to accept—was Howard's insistence on doing his stint at the studios and then quickly departing for New York. It was contrary to Selznick's habit of "collaborating" continually with writer and director.

From 1938 on Howard spent increasingly more time at the five hundred acre farm at Tyringham; he enjoyed working the dairy farm himself, examining the prize herd of Jersey cattle, plowing the fields, gardening, sawing wood.[46] The property is still exceedingly attractive. Once known as the Shaker Meeting House, it sits atop a rise in the Berkshires, a quarter of a mile from Tyringham Civic Center, looking quietly down the open fields to the small cemetery where Howard is buried.

The New York *Times* of August 24, 1939, carried two disturbing stories: one, the first banner headline, was the ironic herald of the European war: "German/Russian Non-Aggression Pact"; the other, subdued across the bottom of the page, was the announcement of a life rudely ended: "Sidney Howard Killed by Tractor on Estate: Playwright is Crushed in Berkshire Garage." The circumstances were bizarre. After a morning's work on "Franklin," an adaptation of the Carl Van Doren biography, Howard went out to harrow a twenty-eight acre field which he had recently bought to extend his property. The *Times* article continues: "Driving alone to the garage a quarter of a mile from his studio in the fields, Mr. Howard entered, turned on the ignition switch of the tractor and cranked it. The machine lurched forward [apparently left in high gear], pinning the playwright against the wall of the structure."

A close friend, Dorothy Thompson, wrote a tribute to Howard in her column for the New York *Herald-Tribune;* she pointed up what was so striking to so many, that a man of peace could be struck down by a blind, mechanical force. Using parallels from the European cinder box, only days from complete explosion, and from Howard's own indictment of war in *Paths of Glory*, she talked movingly of his lifelong battles against aggression—civic, political and military. Along these lines, Howard had recently remarked to her that "the machine takes on a life of its own." The column concluded:

. . . the machine sprang forward, all by itself, without any human will at all, and crushed a man against a wall.

You could write a play about that Sidney.

If the man had not been you.[47]

CHAPTER 2

The Early Work

I Spectacles

IT is not at all unusual that Sidney Howard's first productions for the New York stage were fashionable combinations of romance and spectacle—with various quantities of poetry or lyrical prose. At Harvard he had been greatly influenced by Samuel Hume, whose views of a new stagecraft fitted in well with the popular taste for expansive outdoor pageants. Hume was being recognized as a major force in such theater; exhibitions of his intricate sets were being shown around the country.[1] It had been with the urging of Hume that Howard wrote *The Cranbrook Masque* in 1916 for the private theater of George Booth at his estate in Michigan.[2] The general style for these extravaganzas had been set by Percy MacKaye, whose *Masque of St. Louis* in 1914 had seven thousand participants. Howard's play was essentially an allegory of the poet's quest for beauty. Obvious as these plays were in their easy use of the outdoors space—appearance of the Virgin against the hillside under appropriate lights—they nevertheless offered the young playwright grand opportunities to write in verse. He may well have continued in this popular field if the war had not intervened.

One other opportunity *did* present itself in 1924: Hume commissioned Howard to do the pageant, *Lexington,* for the one hundred and fiftieth anniversary of the Republic. Originally, the assignment had been given to Percy MacKaye but left unfinished. Howard's pageant was presented during the week of June 15, 1925, at Lexington, Massachusetts. The style was the familiar, full-blown spectacle combining many participants and appropriate lyrical declamations. The local paper, however, complained of "red" overtones, perhaps a reference to the last section where modern workers were represented by "groups of vari-

36

colored acrobats in geometrical formations." Even Hume admitted that this part was too much of an abstraction, understandable only to the author.[3]

II *Romances*

By 1921, when Howard's first Broadway venture, *Swords*, was ready to speak to the world, the basic elements of romance and verse were fairly well ingrained in his character.[4] Much of the European time had been spent with foreign languages, medieval literature in particular. He had translated D'Annunzio's *Fedra*, and he was obsessed with the basic story of Dante's Paola and Francesca. Among other related readings were Henry Taylor's *The Medieval Mind* and Henry Adams' *Mont St. Michel and Chartres*. The result for Broadway was a free verse play of twelfth-century Italy, which at least gained Kenneth McGowan's approval since it went beyond the "limits of mechanical realism" into poetry and vision.[5]

The plot, however, is overly involved, concerning, as it does basically, the heroine Fiamma who escapes her imprisonment and seemingly conquers evil at every turn. Each of the four acts follows the same pattern of beginning in comparative calm and ending with a momentous climax as everything centers on Fiamma. Her heroism and saintly manner are in the pattern of the strong woman of character so basic in nearly all of Howard's major plays. Ludwig Lewisohn voiced the objections of the majority in deriding the excessive melodrama and the torrent of words. Citing Howard's "Labor Spy" series, which recently appeared in *The New Republic*, he asked for something closer to home—a coal miner's cottage in the Virginia mountains, for example. He wanted poetic drama, but poetic drama that was *ours*.[6]

Although the experience with *Swords* was sufficient for Howard to give up verse in drama, he nevertheless continued his involvements with romantic subjects. Affected undoubtedly by his translations of plays based on Casanova and Sancho Panza, he tried his hand at a medieval setting in collaboration with Edward Sheldon. *Bewitched* offered an additional challenge in that it combined the past (which Howard was already overly familiar with) and a story of the present.[7] The adopted

device was a play within a play: World War I flyer Jimmie
Stoughton crashes his plane, seeks refuge in an old chateau,
falls asleep under an ancient tapestry, and dreams himself into
the woven tale of the tapestry. It was convenient way of mixing
a fairy tale with some Freudian interpretations. (Freud, by this
time, was becoming familiar on Broadway through the works of
O'Neill, Elmer Rice, and George Kelly.)

Basically, the play is a contest between two kinds of love—the
romantic love of manly adventure and love for a woman. In the
dream idyll Jimmie is put to the test by the Sorcerer in the
Enchanted Wood. Will he stay true to Jeanette, with whom he
has fallen in love, or will he break faith with her before the
dawn? He manages to withstand three explicit temptations involving Freudian confusions of identity; but he is, nevertheless,
restless for the life of adventure. Jeanette shows him how to
escape. In the Epilogue, in present time, the awakened Jimmie
meets the daughter of the Marquis—who, of course, turns out to
be Jeanette.

Sheldon's deeper knowledge of theater was a definite asset;
"with him," wrote Howard, "I got theatre as theatre." In turn,
Sheldon claimed the play was really Howard's.[8] Whatever the
case, the results drew harsh criticism. "A sort of 'Parsifal' on
balloon tires" according to Richard Dana Skinner; "overstated
magic," according to Heywood Broun.[9] Overstated reality, as
well. For example, the initial meeting of our hero with Jeanette
has dialogue of this order: Jeanette: "Oh, you're brave and fine
. . . and you're so clean, too." And later, Jimmie responds, "I've
been wanting romance all my life and here it is." Far more
convincing theatrically is the effective device of having the outline of the aviator at the window (before he breaks into the
chateau) closely resemble a knight in armor.

III   Realism

The way to realism and the final eschewing of old romance
came through Howard's translations of Charles Vildrac's popular
plays of contemporary life—S.S. *Tenacity* (1922) and *Michael
Auclair* (1925).[10] In the postwar French theater Vildrac (1882–
) was hailed as the leader of a new school of realistic drama

which emphasized truthfulness, simplicity, and sincerity. *S.S. Tenacity*, first produced in Paris in 1920, is considered the prime example with its use of ordinary characters and events. Set in a small coastal town, it is a simple tale of two friends waiting in an inn for their ship to take them to Canada and a new life. The more charming one, Bastien, wins the waitress Therese and they run off together. Left now to decide his own fate, which is ironic since it was Bastien who suggested the Canada adventure, Segard the dreamer makes up his own mind to go to Canada and leaves on the *Tenacity*.

Michael Auclair is set in a provincial town prior to 1914. Michael leaves his girl Suzanne to learn the book business in Paris. While away, she marries the soldier Blondeau and is instantly unhappy. Michael tries to reform Blondeau but things get worse. Somehow, the play ends on a note of optimism (characteristic of the 1920's) that Blondeau is not licked yet. A thinner play than *S.S. Tenacity*, it nevertheless had some admirers for the effective language of the French peasants.[11] Both plays are characteristic of the new style in their little braveries. They indicate a reliance on pragmatic rather than heroic action, a quality Howard was to make the essential themes of *They Knew What They Wanted* and *The Silver Cord*.

Vildrac's effect on Howard was electric; he considered the following of Vildrac a new way ("the Vildrac valley"), whereby he could avoid the new fads of expressionism or sensationalism and simply write of everyday men and women. The low-key compromises of little people, making the best of what they have, replaced the literary visions Howard had long nurtured of grand heroics and larger-than-life principals.

IV *The Short Stories*

Sidney Howard published seven short stories in his lifetime. Since six of these appeared between 1920–1925 (and the last in 1929) we can well consider these as products of his apprentice years as a writer. They cover a modest range of subject matter and indicate some experimentation in the form. There are stories about the war, the artist, the deserted but resolute wife, life aboard an ocean steamer; and three attempts at the supernatural

tale. Styles include humor, satire, melodrama, and even one in the
bare naturalistic style made famous by Theodore Dreiser. Interest in fiction continued throughout his mature years as a successful playwright and film scenarist. The letters have continual references to an unfinished novel, *Jacob Ely*, about a
Philadelphia merchant.[12]

V   *"The Stars in Their Courses"* (1920)

"The Stars in Their Courses," the first published story, is,
appropriately enough for a war hero, a war story.[13] Set in Albania,
it concerns the heroics of MacPherson, a volunteer ambulance
driver (like Howard) who hails from Indiana. In contrast to
the customary war yarn, the heroics involve the civilians and not
the military. The story is told by a first-person narrator. Mac-
Pherson, whose "character sticks out of his enthusiasms," brings
a wounded Moslem child and her mother to the unit hospital.
In short order his life is totally wrapped up in their survival:
"here was a new passion, a new devotion, indeed; adventure
enough."

Complications, however, quickly set in: the mother is a Moslem and the father a Christian, which sets off a contention between the Greek Orthodox priests and the Moslem mufti to cure
the girl. MacPherson and the narrator soon find themselves
attacking the Moslem party, whose miraculous "cure" consists
of painfully walking the crippled child and mother away. In
the skirmish, the rescue is accomplished at the cost of a wounded
MacPherson. People like MacPherson, the narrator tells us,
always do the reckless things: "they reckon the act, not the
outcome." The child, ultimately, loses her leg, which merely
adds irony to MacPherson's heroism. The story ends with the
comment that "he had done a rather splendid thing, even if
futile," and one day he would tempt "the lenient god of adventure too far."

The story does manifest some genuine excitement in the
rescue attempt, but it is exceedingly bare in character portrayal.
It would be far better for us to *see* the esteemed elements of
MacPherson's character rather than have the narrator intone
them for us.

VI *"A Likeness of Elizabeth"* (1924)

Howard's interest in the life of painters is best represented by his most successful adaptation, *The Late Christopher Bean* (1932), the charming account of the ironies of artistic success. Equally entertaining and an excellent example of the form is the short story, "A Likeness of Elizabeth."[14] Margot and Paul are two struggling artists in New York, Margot the more accomplished of the two, which adds to their difficulties. To make ends meet she does restorative work for Arnheim, the art dealer. Arnheim craftily puts a bug in her ear by suggesting that she could do a Holbein as well as the master. At first horrified, Margot begins to reconsider when she sees how despondent her husband is. "Obscurity may be nice for violets," she tells herself, "but it's hell on painters." Characteristic of Howard's women, she quickly takes things in stride ("regains her generalship") and takes up Arnheim's offer. The master art forgery begins.

Reminiscent of Henry James' singular ability to give perceptive accounts of states of mind in characters under duress, Howard sketches with great success the conflicting issues running through Margot's mind. How does it feel to be a forger, a criminal—in the art world or anywhere? And what must we say of the art world today? Where is the fairness, the logic? In addition, Howard shows great skill in introducing the lie that Margot will use to account for the increased income. Slowly building up her confidence for the new role she must play, she purchases a new pair of black, luxurious gloves. Later, Paul admires them. Margot replies,

"Something has happened, Paul."
"Something serious?"
She nodded. "I suppose so."
"They're black gloves," Paul observed tensely.
"Has somebody died?"
"Yes," said Margot. "My Aunt Elizabeth died."
She heard herself following Paul's lead quite as though it were her own voice in a high wind and she having nothing whatever to do with it. "My Aunt Elizabeth has died in Philadelphia. You've never heard of her before, have you? I've never seen her myself. But it seems that I'm the only heir."

The structural device is a clever one; the effect is that somehow the lie manifested itself. The pretense also gives her the excuse for doing the Holbein in Philadelphia, where supposedly she must look after her aunt's affairs.

Meanwhile, fellow conspirator Arnheim has a handwriting man in London prepare documentary evidence. He also arranges to have the forged painting, a likeness of the young Queen Elizabeth, "found" in an old barn near Hampton Court. At work in the Philadelphia studio, Margot is engrossed in her subject. Here, again, excellent prose reveals her state of mind: "Holbein possessed her; she possessed Holbein; they absorbed one another. Her hand grew old and tired and ruthlessly wise. Her eyes saw all things expertly and decisively. She learned to drop each morsel of her observations upon the scale of her mind." In four weeks the painting is finished. Arnheim declares it a masterpiece.

Complications, however, begin to accumulate. Phil, an art critic and close friend of the artists, has come out with a definitive study of Holbein. Good suspense is introduced when Phil is asked to authenticate the new "find" arriving from London. In proper melodramatic style (yet, effective) the principals gather to view the painting. Margot's dilemma is well stated: "Margot held her peace, looking down the vista to the glowing small panel at the end where the hard-eyed, divine right of queenship welcomed her out of the face of a little girl and bade her make no sign, betray no fear." Phil, after careful examination, judges the painting to be an original Holbein. He has, evidently, chosen to withhold his reservations until he is able to offer proof of the forgery, which he does in private to Margot. To the great surprise of Margot, he decides to keep the truth to himself. Out of his long-standing admiration for her painting ability and his devotion to beauty, he is determined that the world should have her equal masterpiece to enjoy. "What difference does it make to any of us," he pleads to the startled Margot "even to Holbein himself, so long as it's saved?"

VII *"Transatlantic" (1924)*

The story, "Transatlantic," seems to be Howard's attempt to do the fashionable formless sketch, then popular in the 1920's.[15]

What results is a rather hard to follow series of starts and stops, aimless conversations, abrupt introductions—devices, which are meant to be held together by the mere fact that the passengers are held together on the steamer. The sense of a "drama notebook" is here, as if Howard is trying out random bits of dialogue. However, the required degrees of cleverness to hold such loose elements together are not really evident.

The story opens with Jennie Watson, thirty-eight, going out on a tender at Cherbourg to board the steamer. She seems forceful and direct: "Her mind was filled with an energy at once jaunty and leonine." True to the picture of a dynamic, modern woman, she wastes little time once aboard the ship; she introduces herself to Harry and to the Englishman, Burleigh. Other meetings, with new, different sets of characters also take place. The style, confusing at first, provides a number of brief sections, each introducing new characters and abrupt conversations. Jennie and Harry gradually emerge as the central characters. We learn that she is going home to her husband and children, that basically she is her own woman, that, moreover, she likes Prohibition since it provides a ready way to meet men. A number of incidentals come to mind, deliberately sketchy. Together Jennie and Harry visit the engine room, and reflections follow on the energy below decks compared to the frivolous life above. Obviously, this is strongly reminiscent of Eugene O'Neill's success of two years earlier, *The Hairy Ape*, in which Mildred is similarly struck by the brutish energy of Yank as he stokes the furnaces.

At times, the descriptive terms are precise and imaginative. Deck chairs are "folded away into the angular formlessness of their night's repose." At other times the cleverness is simply precocious: "Sea-going swimming pools can be Homerically tempestuous." Almost as bothersome is the occasional French word given a merciless phonetic spelling, "murcee."

VIII "Mrs Vietch: A Segment of Biography" (1924)

By the mid 1920's, Theodore Dreiser was well established as the controversial exponent of literary naturalism. *Sister Carrie* (1900) and *The Genius* (1915) had made their stormy appearances, and the pattern of depressing, seedy lives of economic and sexual despair was readily known and available. Howard became one of the loyal followers with "Mrs. Vietch: A Segment of Biography."[16] The title alone suggests the mechanistic, generalizing way of considering individual characters; we have the immediate strong feeling that we are reading a dossier or a numbered file folder in a social welfare bureau. The fast pace of the narration contributes to the effect. What should be "dramatics of the moment" become resumé, and the result is that the credibility for the events is reduced. We seem to be on the outside of the story, and only rarely and awkwardly are we inside and somewhat involved.

The story is set in Alameda, California. Ruby is the somewhat ugly duckling daughter whose chances at first seem slim compared to the prettier Pearl. However, stolid and reliable Mr. Vietch comes into their lives and he marries Ruby and they settle down in their own house. Six years pass, Baby Thelma arrives, all seems well, and then suddenly Mr. Vietch abandons the family and sails away. In typical Howard fashion, Ruby rises to the occasion: she has mother and Pearl move in with her to save money, and the two sisers begin "careers" of earnest sewing at home. Ruby's determination seems to be holding the family together.

What follows next in the history of Ruby is a quick series of melodramatic events. Pearl marries and moves to Los Angeles. Question again arises as to whether Ruby can still make ends meet. She rents one room out. Apparently saved again, she is almost immediately plunged into the worst despair. Thelma has the scarlet fever and the five-week quarantine prevents Ruby from working. An excellent scene is then carefully developed which dramatizes her helplessness when she tries to secure an increase from the people she sews for. It is probably the most effective scene in the story. The nadir, however, is reached when Thelma dies and Ruby's mother moves to Los Angeles.

The pathetic becomes melodramatic again when Mr. Vietch returns. With a few other roomers in tow, she musters her bravery again and orders Vietch to leave. At the end, she resolutely decides to sell her hair—her crowning glory. By this time, almost thriving on adversity, she seems to be growing stronger than ever. Nevertheless, in standard naturalistic fashion, the reader is left on the last page with only the bleak record of a dismal life. "So her story ended a bit less than a year after it began and she was 27 years old and her life lay before her empty as a tin can thrown over a fence to rust in a vacant lot."

IX *"The God They Left Behind Them"* (1924)

The story, "The God They Left Behind Them," represents Howard's first attempt at the supernatural tale.[17] Obviously inspired by the Jonathan Edwards House in Stockbridge, Massachusetts, it is set in an equally old house once owned by one of his disciples. Constantia and her writer husband Oliver Ramsay reopen the old house and modernize it. Their publisher, Caxton—what better name for a "producer" of type—spends the weekend with them. They are all a bit taken by their neighbor, Ruth Wilmot, the local historical society curator, who seems to have spent much of her twenty-nine years "watching out" for the house. Her ancestor was another disciple of Edwards. The eeriness increases when Oliver sees Ruth apparently praying on the lawn for the house.

Evidently, Ruth's task seems to be one of protecting Edwards' "domain" from intruders: directly she warns Caxton of Edwards' anger and the danger to the Ramsays. All of this is done in a kind of maniac torrent of words. Edwards seems to be a contemporary of hers; she relates how he was driven out of Northampton with his fire and brimstone sermons and came to Stockbridge. When Caxton protests, she counters with "Don't you know that gods can't die." Left to himself, Caxton considers the issues. However, what should have been stimulating psychological questions and answers to himself about Edwards, the New England puritan heritage and what it portends, becomes instead a rather obvious author's analysis and exposition entirely from the outside. The climax is reached when they decide to exorcise the spirits from the house. Candles are lit; Edwards books are thrown into the fire. A frantic Ruth storms into the house, and then a presence seems to overwhelm them all. "Like a throbbing in the ears" it came on them "like heat." The

Ramsays fly out of the house. Caxton hears a voice—the words are Edwards—"I am that I am . . . I am that I am." Caxton rushes out. At dawn the next morning Ruth comes out with a valise and addresses Caxton who has waited through the night. "You needn't be angry any more. You needn't be lonely. They won't come here any more, but I shall. I shall come often."

Howard's failure here is common to many writers. So much attention is given to convincing us of the *meaning* of the horror that we are never moved by the horror itself. Henry James, in a classic literary "discussion" with Robert Louis Stevenson on the use of the supernatural, pointed out that the primary task is to believe in the terror, to create that mood, as in "The Turn of the Screw" (1898), and not to rely alone on powders and extrinsic devices, as in the "Strange Case of Dr. Jekyll and Mr. Hyde" (1886).[18] The Jamesian advice, quite simply, is that if you succeed in making the reader imagine the horror (rather than knowing it all) you then have a continually provocative tale of the supernatural. Here, in contrast, the mood is overly contrived; and since the characters lack dimension, we are never convinced of what they believe or see. We have the feeling that Howard uses the elements of a supernatural tale really to do other things—to say things about New England backgrounds and their influences today. In that sense, a careful reading of the story does reveal interesting aspects of his sense of the past.

X *"Such Women as Ellen Steele"* (1925)

"Such Women as Ellen Steele" is another story which attempts to evoke a spiritual presence.[19] This time we have a deceased actress, Ellen Steele, barely a year in her grave, who apparently is determined to affect the life of her husband, George Kinkead. We must certainly give Howard credit for devising one of the strangest ways for her to accomplish her purpose. Kinkead, a highly respected Bostonian, living quietly in a brownstone on Marlborough Street, has a recurring dream in which he sits up as in a theater and claps his hands wildly. The neurologist Adams is baffled by all this and speculates that it must relate to his wife of sixteen years who gave up a promising acting career when she married him. We learn that her life seemed to end, in a sense, at marriage: "She bloomed to be enjoyed, if ever a woman did, and then came the man who could not enjoy her without cutting her off from all that gave her life."

As things get worse for Kinkead, Adams decides to spend a night in his home and to watch this strange phenomenon for himself. A number of times during the night Adams sees Kinkead go through the same routine: he sits up, claps wildly with his eyes open in a kind of "ecstatic delight." Each time the seizure ends as a kind of release, "like the letting go of a power." Months pass, long stays in hospitals follow; and soon the seizures become more and more frequent, wasting him entirely. Finally, as if "at perpetual play, watching and applauding," Kinkead dies of exhaustion.

Why and how it happened are discussed by the narrator and Adams. They speculate that Ellen's ghost must have wanted to have her as an actress again, that a tremendous force (her great desire) finally broke its bounds and returned. She had evidently restrained herself for the sixteen years of the marriage—and then death released her. "She was an actress," Adams said. "Such women have vigor in them."

XI "*The Homesick Ladies*" (1929)

"The Homesick Ladies," actually a lesser story than some of Howard's others, was awarded second prize in the O. Henry Memorial Award competition for 1929.[20] Surprisingly, despite the two thousand entries and numerous famous names, the story seemed to impress the judges. Perhaps, this tells us something of contemporary taste—or contemporary judges. The elements are novel enough; but as another ghost story it also falls wide of the mark. The effect is of some one attempting to be ghostlike and mysterious by simply saying it. We miss the sense of the unbelievable, the unexplainable intruding into everyday life.

Horace Rideout decides to sell the family house in Maine and move to Boston. He writes to his two half-sisters and tells them his plans. Bessie, in real estate in New York, a ponderous woman at three hundred pounds ("Madame of New York Real Estate"), arrives without notice. The other sister, in Rome, is not heard from. Bessie experiences waves of homesickness in seeing the old house again, an impressive Georgian mansion.[21] We also learn that Bessie once had a romantic attachment with neighbor Crandall, now a widower. The immediately following scene is an abrupt introduction of a strange, tired woman to the rear door of the Rideout home. She is befriended by the servants, and it does not take us very long to realize that she is probably the other sister, Maisie. Here, of course, the elements of coincidence and possible suspense are barely convincing. Frankly, we do not receive the waves of sentimental relief ("I've come home at last") that her melodramatic return to the family is scheduled to bring.

In the family reunion it becomes apparent that Maisie is thoroughly confused and believes she is a child again. We learn that she had also been in love with Crandall years ago in Vienna. Suddenly, Maisie is missing, and a telegram from the *Berengaria* at sea arrives: "Don't sell, I'm coming home, Maisie." When the mystification (or what passes for it) is eventually lifted, they conclude that Maisie must have died at sea and that they have been entertaining her ghost. Bessie ventures the thought that it must be the power of homesickness that brought her home. In a last—and almost incredible—scene we are given a picture of two little girls climbing the stairs slowly to bed, saying "good-night," as the story ends. Here, as in the Ellen Steele story, the supernatural seems to be merely an excuse for doing something else. Nostalgia seems to be Howard's main concern, which in itself works well enough. I doubt, however, if contemporary readers would agree with one of the judges that the final scene is "hauntingly lovely."

CHAPTER 3

They Knew What They Wanted
(1924)

THE title of Howard's most famous play, *They Knew What They Wanted*, tells nearly as much about the author as it does about the play.[1] Ever forthright and well known for his dynamic, positive manner, Howard succeeded admirably in fashioning a play which champions the same virtues. A matter-of-fact certainty and blunt pragmatism rule the lives of his three principals. What finally resolves the issues at the end of the play is simply the agreement *not* to resolve them at all, that is, not to resolve them in the usual searing probes into human nature. Resolution here is simply a comic standstill, an acceptance of things as they seem to be for better or for worse. This, in effect, is what differentiates the play from that other success of 1924, O'Neill's *Desire Under the Elms*, with which it is often compared. Amazingly similar in plot, they do, nevertheless, derive from two distinctly different concepts. O'Neill writes a modern tragedy; Howard writes a modern comedy.

The play is set in the Napa Valley in California, an area which the young Howard knew very well. The grape growing communities fill the low hills and wide valleys north of San Francisco Bay, providing an excellent choice for a story about essentially simple, warm-hearted people. At first Howard had the thought of writing a short story about an Italian who wanted to establish a dynasty like the Goulds or Astors. Experiments in trying to approximate the rich Italian dialect in words convinced him that it would be better as a spoken piece for the theater.[2] And, of course, the conception of Tony as the prosperous, middle-aged owner of the vineyard, never developed into a story of economic power; Tony remains a modestly content rancher. He does, however, have a great style. Howard describes his first

49

entrance: "Magnificently Tony enters from the bedroom. He is stout, floridly bronzed, sixty years old, vigorous, jovial, simple, and excitable. His great gift is for gesture. Today we meet him in his Sunday best, a very brilliant, purple suit with a more than oriental waistcoat which serves to display a stupendous gold watch chain. He wears a boiled shirt, an emerald-green tie, and a derby hat. He carries his new patent-leather shoes in his hand. He seems to be perspiring rather freely." The "Sunday best" is to meet his mail-order bride, Amy, who is arriving today from San Francisco. We learn that Joe, his young and handsome assistant, has actually written the letters for him and that it is his picture, not Tony's, that has won the older man a bride.

These complexities are enough to provide the basis for the comedy of confusion and discovery which fills Act One. The initial characterizations of Tony and his partner in duplicity, the carefree Joe, are exceptionally well done. The introductory scenes are cleverly arranged, with Father McKee, the local Catholic priest, serving as a catalyst to bring out the situation. He is there to question the propriety of such a wedding under such unusual circumstances; primarily, he's concerned about the age difference. Interesting ambiguities instantly set in: Tony is anxious to have Joe leave after the wedding because of the deception; Father McKee, not knowing the entire story, believes the departure is simply a practical precaution since Joe is widely known as a lusty romancer. To Father McKee's opinion that Tony should have found someone in his own parish, Tony has a ready reply: "Joe is sleepin' with evra one." To the basic question of Father McKee: "There ain't no good in no old man marryin' with no young woman," Tony has the best answer: "You think any-body marry with old woman?"

Tony's deepest feelings are honestly expressed in a winning simplicity: "She [Amy] is like a rose, all wilt. You puttin' water on her an' she come out most beautiful. I'm goin' marry with my Amy, Padre, an' I don' marry with nobody else." Tony had seen her once in San Francisco as a waitress, never talked to her but simply got her address. Somehow, as we know Tony better, the utter foolishness of his courtship seems almost an irrelevant issue. The character is so well drawn that we never ask the wrong (or right) questions. He never married earlier, he tells

Father McKee, because he was too poor; he didn't want a wife "for mak' her work all da time." That would be no good, "Da's mak' her no more young no more prett.'" But now that Prohibition has come, which is "dam' fool law," since "God mak' dees country for growin' da grape," Tony has become prosperous and can now afford a wife. It is hard to refute his logic. His plans are, he concludes, "fine for God an' evrabody! I tell you, Padre, Tony knows w'at he want!"

Tony leaves for the station to meet Amy, but somehow they miss each other and Amy arrives at the ranch on her own. Immediately we sense the presence of another person who seems to know what she wants. At first angry at not being met, she quickly alters her mood before Father McKee and Joe: "All right, then, I'll forgive you. That's the way I am. Forgive and forget! I always believe in letting bygones be bygones." In her own way she astounds them; she is all that Tony had said of her, very pretty, small, with golden hair and a "face like morning sunshine." Howard describes her as shining "with an inner, constitutional energy. Her look is, to be sure, just a little tired. She probably is not more than twenty-two or -three, but she seems older. Her great quality is definiteness. It lends pathos to her whole personality." She also talks along at a rather brisk pace, perhaps to keep up her courage. Alone now with Joe when the others have to leave, she sets off an excellent comic scene by assuming that Joe is Tony. In Joe's rather natural reluctance to explain we have the sufficient delays for many double meanings and comic lines.

An uproar quickly ensues with the excited arrival of Tony who has been in a serious auto accident. They bring him in on a bench, both legs in compound fractures; otherwise, he's as talkative as ever and full of apologies for Amy. At first horrified when she finally learns who Tony really is, she quickly calms down and tries to take the situation in hand. Here, of course, we meet the typical Howard heroine again. Somewhat like the pathetic Mrs. Vietch (in the short story of the same year) she pulls herself up out of seeming adversity and confusion and takes a stand. While the others stare in admiration, she firmly announces her decision as the first act curtain falls. "No. I ain't going. Why should I go? I like the country. This place suits me

all right. It's just what I was looking for. I'm here and I might
as well stick. I guess he ain't so bad, at that. I guess I could
have done a lot worse. If he wants to marry me, I'm game. I'm
game to see it through. It's nice up here."

The wedding takes place; the festivities go on long into the
night despite the seriousness of Tony's condition and the doctor's
protestations. He will, however, be laid up at least six months. Joe
consoles Tony with his "philosophy of women," emphasizing
that they need caring for—"knockin' around just raises hell with
a girl"—since they can't stand the rough times a man can take.
To Tony Joe seems very smart about women. Amy, however, is
obviously bothered by Joe's presence, and it quickly becomes
apparent that she is trying to deny the effect he has on her. The
scene develops well between the three of them: Tony is pressing
an expensive set of earrings on his Amy; Joe is trying somehow
to back off, reduce his presence; Amy, tearful, still snaps at Joe
—perhaps again to keep up her courage. Tony is determined now
that Joe stay on even though he would rather leave. Amy attempts
to feign indifference. They continue to spar with each other
when alone, which increases the audience's anticipation of
things to come. This scene, the seduction scene, which closes the
second act, is obviously not an easy scene to write. We must be
convinced in so many lines, movements, and stage business that
their coming together is completely inevitable. It is made to work
by the clever running out of nearly all of Amy's desperate
thoughts—why she left San Francisco, what she is determined to
do here for Tony, even without love. "I got all I bargained for,"
she tells Joe, "and then some. I'm fixed. I'm satisfied. I didn't
come up here . . . like I did . . . looking for love . . . or . . . or . . .
anything like that." She finally softens toward Joe when he
admits he never knew of the photo deception. And in her
contriteness (or weariness) she stumbles into his arms—and
rather believably, passion quickly takes hold. The act ends, as
he determinedly runs after her out of the house.

Three months later, as Act Three opens, we find the house
markedly changed by the presence of a woman. Curtains, lamp
shades, some embroidered works—all indicate a kind of domestic
tranquility. While the others talk politics, Amy seems privately
content: "Well, the world may need reforming but I got no

kick." Quickly we learn in the doctor's accusation of Joe, that Amy is pregnant; and perhaps the best thing to do is for the two to leave. Amy takes the news as a kind of moral judgment: "If you go wrong, you're sure to get it sooner or later, I got it sooner." The attitude is completely characteristic of Amy in her rather pitiless view of life and things. Take everything as it comes seems to be her philosophy of life. Apparently, there is no other course but to leave together, which they agree reluctantly to do. The traumatic effect on Tony is well prepared for with the following dialogue:

AMY: Joe's going away.
TONY: He's no' goin' without sayin' goo'-by?
AMY: I dunno. . . . Maybe he is. . . .
TONY: That boy mak' me verra unhappy. I been lovin' Joe like he was my own son an' he's goin' away like dat. He's no good.
AMY: People who ain't no good ain't worth worrying about. The thing to do is let 'em go and forget 'em.
TONY: Da's no' so easy like you think, Amy. I been lovin' Joe like my own son.
AMY: Joe ain't no worse than other people I could mention.
TONY: I love Joe but he don' love me.
AMY: I love you, Tony! I love you!
TONY: I know, Amy, I know.
AMY: And you ain't never going to believe that I do again.

This scene, of course, becomes the most challenging for Howard. When Tony finally learns the truth he goes completely berserk, even accusing her of being a whore. In another sense, the excitement of the scene adds up to good sentiment and melodrama as Amy pleads in her defense and gradually wears Tony down. Tony and Joe first scuffle over the gun on the wall and finally Tony is quieted. He now sees what must be done: he begs Amy to stay with him and have her baby. After all, it "ees good sense! Eees w'at is evrabody wantin' here! You an' Joe an' me!" His conviction mounts as his anger subsides; there's no denying the eminent practicality of his suggestion, which of course holds the entire meaning of the play. Moral judgments aside, Tony has his own reassurance in answer to Amy's confession of guilt: "What you done was mistake in da head, not in da heart.... Mistake in da head is no matter." And so—with Joe's departure—the comedy comes to a happy ending.

I *Sources*

There were many speculations about the source of the plot. Although Howard denied "hotly" its relationship to the legend of Paola and Francesca, there are still the obvious parallels. In Dante's *Divine Comedy* the story is related of the deformed Giancotto who has Paola woo Francesca for him by proxy. Following the marriage, the husband discovers their attachment and kills them both. In the Preface to the published edition, Howard admitted his reliance on Wagner's great romantic opera, *Tristan und Isolde*, and particularly the earlier medieval tale: "It [the play] is shamelessly, consciously, and even proudly derived from the legend of Tristran and Yseult, and the difference between the legend of Tristran and Yseult and that of Paola and Francesca is simply that the Italian wronged husband killed everybody in sight while his northern counterpart forgave everybody—which amounts to the monumental difference between a bad temper and tolerance."[3] A marvelous explanation; and obviously written in Howard's characteristic high, buoyant style —the style, incidentally, of many of his personal letters.

The difference, then, between the two legends is that all important one to Howard, the tolerance of the wronged husband. Even though in bare outline the Paola story is actually closer to the facts of Howard's play, it is the Tristran story ending that concerns Howard. According to the original medieval romance Tristran has the charge to woo Yseult (Isolde) for his lord. By accident they drink a love potion and become lovers. Exiled to another land, he lies dying and asks for Yseult to heal him. She arrives with her husband, who miraculously had come to unite the unhappy lovers, but they find Tristran dead. Forgiveness, understanding—not a mistake of "da heart"—underlie both stories. It is as if Howard is saying in his modern morality tale that we all make mistakes, that circumstances often mislead us, but that we must not be judged too harshly.

There is a touch of the naturalistic philosophy in the plight of Amy and Joe, somewhat reminiscent of Dreiser's trapped people—caught not so much by their own internal weaknesses

but by the inexorable forces of the world they live in. Much of
the play is given to the 1920 context, Prohibition, the IWW
(International Workers of the World) issues in particular with
the attendant hates and violence. Joe sings at the beginning of
the play, "Remember," an IWW song:[4]

> "We speak to you from jail to-day,
> Two hundred union men,
> We're here because the bosses' laws
> Bring slavery again."

The opening, lengthy scene of Act Three is a full scale discussion among Father McKee, Joe, and Tony on government
today and the threat from radicals such as Joe. With Father
McKee on one side and Joe on the other and Tony somewhat in
the middle ("I don' want changin' nothing.") we get a rather
accurate picture of the turbulent times. The young man of little
means is restless with the capitalistic structure, the man of the
church wants stability, and the happy winegrower makes money
by the bushel.

FATHER McKEE: You radicals, Joe, you're always an' forever hol-
lerin' an' carryin' on 'bout your rights. How about your duties? There
ain't no one to prevent your doin' your duties but you ain't never
done 'em in your life.
JOE: I'm savin' my duties for the brotherhood of man.
TONY: Dio mio!
FATHER McKEE: You're talkin' a lot of balderdash. Mind your own
business an' leave the brotherhood of man to me. Brothers is *my* job.
TONY: You think evrabody's goin' be brother like dat an' don'
scrap no more? Eees crazy idea! You ain't got no good sense, Joe,
you an' dos goddam Wobblies.

Essentially, however, Joe *is* the radical of the 1920's. "Maybe I
don't mean nothin' at all. Maybe I'm just restless an' rarin' to go."
There are scraps, like the dock strike at San Pedro, that he
should get into. "The only freedom we got left" Joe tells the
others, "is the freedom to choose which one of our rights we'll
go to jail for." This, then, is the kind of anti-hero of the times
so popular in contemporary literature. Match Joe up with the

hapless Amy and we have a worthy pair for sympathy—not censure.

We stress "pathetic" with Amy only in the sense that she can really do so very little to order her life. Within a rather narrow box she struts her independence but it is always, no matter what, still a box. Her great strength is her pragmatism, the undeniable power to make the best of things. "Well, the world may need reforming," she bravely tells the philosophers as she joins them, "but I got no kick. The grapes is near ripe and ready for picking. The nights is getting longer, the mornings is getting colder, and Tony's getting better. Down town they're putting up the posters for the circus and I hear the show's going into winter quarters just the other side of Napa. I guess that's all the remarks I got to make now." Howard admitted to Barrett Clark that this opening scene of Act Three was what he liked best in the play—the chance for Amy in her simple way to put down the others (Clark, p. 202)

II *The Critics*

There was no doubt, of course, as to what elements in the play pleased the public most. Grim feminine energy—in the 1920's— would always have a great following. The emancipated young woman, represented on the stage by O'Neill's Pulitzer Prize winner, *Anna Christie* (1921), was still very much on people's mind. The notices for Howard were nearly all enthusiastic. Heywood Broun wrote that it was "a soul-rousing play out of American life. Comedy and tragedy struggle for the soul of this story, and it is no weak-kneed concession that comedy plunges through."[5] Similar views were expressed by Alexander Woolcott: "*They Knew What They Wanted* is a true, living, salty comedy . . . a colorful piece cut from the genuine fabric of American life. It is one of those comedies which move uneasy on the edge of tragedy."[6] The dividing line between comedy and tragedy became a familiar referent. "Such hard punches as it bestows," wrote Percy Hammond, "are softened by the mellow four-ounce gloves of humor and sentiment."[7] There were those reviewers, of course, who were reserved in their judgments. George Jean Nathan said the play was a pleasant, sophisticated comedy, ably produced and well acted, but not entirely the great American masterpiece, as some believed. It was, nevertheless, a "praise-worthy attempt."[8]

By the time Howard's play had toured the country and been produced in London, it had become something of a sensation. The production was one of the first major American plays to come to London, and in many quarters Howard's reputation was second only to O'Neill, which some denied. The London critic for *Theatre World* wrote, "There is a restraint and balance about the writing of the play so remote from the usual mechanicalized American sub-stuff."[9] Another *Theatre World* critic seemed cheered by his "relief" in finding that "its final message of forgiveness" rescued the play from being a "sex play," evidently the lowest current category in London. On the other hand, some American critics felt the play wasn't "rescued" enough from the subject of sex. Arthur Hornblow said it was "an unusually well-constructed play, smudged up with repellent situations."[11] Hornblow went even further and wrote an editorial five months later criticizing on moral grounds the choice of *They Knew What They Wanted* for the Pulitzer Prize. He cited the actual wording of the instructions to the Pulitzer Prize Committee: in effect, to choose literature which "raises the standards of good morals, good taste, and good manners."[12]

III *The New Realism*

The war against false morality was well fought by Howard that year in curious conjunction with another drama which further questioned traditional attitudes. The other play was O'Neill's *Desire Under the Elms,* which featured a similar adulterous conspiracy of young lovers at the expense of the older husband.[13] The two playwrights' differing accomplishments along this one common theme of seduction reveal interesting facets in the range of theatrical possibilities. The results, of course, mirror the thinking of the times. The wave of the new realism, inspired by Charles Vildrac and other Europeans, was well on its way in sweeping away the outmoded Victorian attitudes. A brief comparison of the two plays is a good illustration of theater coming of age, pointing up, as it does, Howard's unique comic spirit.

Desire Under the Elms, set in 1850 on a New England farm, tells the story of old Ephraim Cabot who takes a young second wife, Abby. Through careful scheming she engineers the seduction of Cabot's young son, Eben, and produces a child of this union to her husband. In his great vanity, he never doubts that it is his. Abby, fearful that she has lost Eben because of the child, kills the baby, believing it will restore Eben to her. The play ends with the apprehension of Eben and Abby by the local authorities. In a comparison of the two plays, we see first of all a similar setting, a farm. Both playwrights give extensive stage directions: carefully pointing up the grape vines in their changing color in the Howard play, and the overhanging, oppressive elm boughs (perhaps symbolic of fate) in the O'Neill play. The emphasis with Howard is on the simple, good life of the Italo-Americans; O'Neill emphasizes the hard, rigorous life of the Yankee farmer. We are not then surprised that the Howard play becomes romantic, sentimental, optimistic. O'Neill stresses harsh realism, pessimism. Whereas the resolution of Howard's plot follows a kind of moral goodness, O'Neill's plot demands more imperatives—the essential differences between the pathetic and the tragic.

The relationship to God on the part of Tony and Cabot, the two wronged husbands, is another interesting comparison. Tony berates himself for his ill luck, the accident, and has doubts about Amy's real affection. In rather standard, formal church fashion, he blames his misfortune on a providential, angry God: "I been verra bad sinner an' God is goin' get me for sure! He's broke both my legs already an' he's not finish' with me yet! God is no cheap fella, Joe." We smile indulgently at much of this, the penitent attitude being almost universally familiar, even with the large majority of good/bad men not so formally church bound as Tony. These are good echoes of the human condition. Other issues, however, characterize old Cabot in his relationship to God. A man of his times (1850's), he appears more thoroughly immersed in the Puritan theology of an Angry God. We sense a kind of demoniac Jonathan Edwards in Cabot's incessant bible quoting and ravings.

Appropriate differences also exist between Abby and Amy, the essential differences between a kind of reduced, limited human order, and perhaps some promise of the future with Amy. Abby is all flesh and desire, impetuous, scheming—in sum, actually stupid. It is difficult to have much sympathy for her individually. If anything, we are affected by the type. Amy, on the other hand, is quick, resourceful, a kind of pragmatic maid-in-the-woods who will somehow manage. The entire point of Howard's comic idyll is summed up in Joe's words on Amy: "If she's not good, she wants to be." What we have then, in effect, is "a kind of philosophical middle ground"—to quote Joseph Wood Krutch. Howard's approach is "freshly American"; it is a highly welcome "qualified optimism," Krutch continues, in stark contrast to more somber foreign influences, so fashionable in the 1920's. Moreover, "his evocation of a mood midway between tragedy and comedy had the effect of suggesting sincerity," the one quality which so marks Howard—man and author.[14]

CHAPTER 4

Plays of the 1920's ... The Silver Cord

I Lucky Sam McCarver *(1925)*

WHAT can one make of a play that has a disastrously short run, receives high critical acclaim, and is thought by the playwright to be his best play?[1] True, the situation is not unique; it has happened before with some of the world's greatest literature. Usually the fault is with an audience not ready for a great work of art. Although, quite frankly in this case, Howard is the first to admit, half humorously, that the play is deficient. "Indeed, the only difference I can discern between my play and several masterpieces is one of artistic merit."[2] What makes the play of great value in the overall estimation of Howard's career are the high hopes he had for the work (well expressed in the Preface to the published play), together with reminders of the apparent realities of theatrical success. We have the chance here to see rather well into Howard's dramatic imagination. And what is even more advantageous, our analysis, as we come to it, points up what may be the substantial basis for the successful plays.

The character of Sam McCarver brings to mind another mysterious man of the underworld in the fiction of 1925—the nefarious Jay Gatsby of Scott Fitzgerald. Although *The Great Gatsby* appeared six months earlier there is no reason to suppose a heavy Howard reliance on the novel. Certainly the type—the underworld man of power—was common enough in the headlines of the 1920's. Howard's play opens on New Year's Eve in the Club Tuileries, a New York nightclub owned by Sam McCarver. The various attendants and hangers-on are well described, and we have a convincing picture of the seamier side of the entertainment world. We learn that Sam cares for Carlotta Ashe, a wealthy and attractive socialite divorcee. Sam is introduced as a man of few refinements but with an "instinctive wariness" and "innate force." He speaks with "a mixture of Broadway, East Side, and the Ould Country." His closeness with Sergeant Horan of the Police and other authorities of the Prohibition Unit quickly reminds us of the curious yet practical ironies of the Speakeasy Age. They all, of course, have a drink together in the club.

Preparations are underway for the festivities. There is some talk about Monty Garside, a wealthy but noisy patron who is behind in his account. They decide to give him a bad table too close to the band. Sam's partners are wary of the boss' relations with Carlotta. She's notoriously wild. "God damn it, Sam!— she ain't good enough for you!" they remind him. Sam counters by saying he needs her to get up in the world; he is not a "romantic man." The Carlotta crowd, which includes Garside, becomes louder and more boisterous in the box outside the office. We learn that Carlotta met Garside in Atlantic City and that they took a taxi into the city. Sam is reluctant to believe all the stories available about the two of them. He describes Carlotta as a "masterpiece . . . centuries to produce her . . . a sort of danger-signal which nature hangs out to warn a race of its decadence." To quiet things in the club Sam orders that his private box in the balcony be given to Carlotta and her friends, even if it seems to spoil his own plans with her for the evening. The manner whereby this bit of business is done establishes Sam as very much like Gatsby in his feigned extreme reserve and politeness. He seems to be trying to outdo the socialites, particularly now when they are half-drunk and he remains coldly sober and in command. Sam greets Carlotta calmly despite the ruckus:

SAM: I'm glad to see you here, Mrs. Ashe. I hoped you were going to be my guest tonight.
CARLOTTA: What was I to do with poor Monty? Look how tight he is! Isn't it too vile of him!
SAM: You're very beautiful to-night.
CARLOTTA: Thank you. Come and enjoy me while I last.

The two have a kind of sparring conversation in his office as he talks of himself and his hopes while she rather obviously plays with him. He might marry, Sam says seriously. "It's a perfectly poisonous idea," she answers. "I shan't love you any more if you get married!" Nevertheless, he does propose to her and she neatly evades the issue for now. She returns to join the others in the box—and then a great commotion lets loose. Jimmie, a jealous and recently fired employee, shoots and kills Monty Garside. Over the uproar, a very cool Sam quickly takes control. He "arranges" things to look as if Garside pulled a gun and that he had to kill him in self-defense. He sends Jimmie away, calls in Sergeant Horan, and calmly gives the new version of the entire fracas. Of course, everyone corroborates the story, and the act ends with Sam as a kind of resolute hero.

The second act, set in Sam's luxurious Park Avenue apartment three months later, quickly informs us that Carlotta has married him, probably out of gratitude (strange as it seems) for his saving her from scandal in the Garside shooting. A guarded kind of love seems to exist between the two. There is also some financial blackmailing going on by her stockbroker, Burton, who wants Carlotta's help in getting into a McCarver million-dollar investment. Burton threatens to reveal the truth about Garside. Sam's mixing with the socialite world runs hot and cold. Whereas Carlotta's cousin, Archie, foretells disaster, her aunt, the Princess Strá, is fascinated: "He's the most distinguished thing you've ever done. He reeks of the underworld!" The intent here is to give us a modish picture of one of the mad matrons of the 1920's; however the characterization is very thin and relies simply on generalities about the type. Most of the act is taken up with Sam and Carlotta, mostly heated disagreements and very few agreements. Each seems to be trying to use the other. Sam wants her family name for the new investment scheme. She agrees as long as Burton is included.

A.   The Smart Set in Venice

The scene now shifts for the third act to Venice, to the Palazza Strá where the Princess lives surrounded by the international set. Among her house guests are Sam and Carlotta, Archie, and Carlotta's ex-husband, Carter Ashe. This arrangement is obviously overcontrived; Carter becomes the intellectual spokesman for the author and explains too much about everything. An added trick, for whatever irony it will bring, is to have Carter immediately understand Sam and vice versa. Carter gives his analysis of the underworld czar: "You've thought more about the universe than any man I know. Only you call it 'Your Career' or 'Life,' or something equally personal. You look on the universe as a series of puddles, each one bigger than the last and each one made for you to jump in and be Big Frog. Well, the universe has a queer way of conforming to what any man wants of it—up to a certain point." Sam rejects the advice. Others join the set, and Howard attempts a Philip Barry kind of smart talk; which, however, is never really brittle or clever enough. Much of it sails over Sam's bewildered head. Carlotta and her husband come to verbal blows again: she accuses him of being an "innocent," of boring her. "I wonder," she says, "how much there is to choose between my 'tribe' and you. . . . I've never seen any tribe that wasn't somehow better than the man who was too good for it." Sam, disgusted, plans to pack up and leave.

The last act is in New York in Carlotta's Upper West Side apartment. Seven months have passed and she is noticeably ill. A somewhat altered Sam is also introduced; he is dressed well, has gained some dignity (all unexplained) and "grown just a little ridiculous about it." Everything is falling apart for Carlotta— her health, her finances—although Sam has no plans to divorce her. She seems to be mustering all her bravado and cynicism in her refusal of his offer of money. "You're a go-getter," she tells him. "I'm a runner-away." A few more bravados, and eventually her heart gives out and she dies.

Despite its early close, many critics praised the play, apparently seeing essential things about Howard in the play. Montrose Moses said it was one of Howard's most distinguished dramas, and reported that respected Broadway critics thought it should be kept alive in repertory.[3] Burns Mantle seriously considered it for one of the ten best of the year in his annual compilations.[4] John Mason Brown said the play is "the key to Mr. Howard's best abilities. It is the most personal of his plays in that it is freest from compromises with theatrical effectiveness. And it is the least obvious."[5] Whatever Brown's real critical intent, he

does point to the essential problems. As a "key" to Howard
what does the play open up? Can "theatrical effectiveness" be so
easily dispensed with? And, is obscurity really a virtue? We
needn't look very far for the materials of discussion since Howard's Preface explicitly explains his entire approach to the work.

B. *The Preface*

The Preface is a major document since it not only discusses
Lucky Sam McCarver but also has the fullest statement on his
well known view that plays exist primarily for actors. Howard
says the play failed because he was attempting dramatic biography, "detached episodes" in the lives of two representative,
divergent New York types. The self-accusation seems to imply
the truth that dramatic biography without theatrical devices is
fairly limp stuff for the legitimate stage. We watch without getting involved. Of course, the further fault is that even as dramatic
biography the play seems embarrassingly incomplete. We never
seem really to know enough about the principals. Howard
explains:

Once I had decided to write this play, I determined to see it through
on its own line to its own logical destination. I deliberately stacked
my cards against my two characters. I gave my man an overweening
ambition for material success. I gave my woman an indomitable
passion for material pleasure. I made my man both hale and shrewd.
I gave my woman a body as inept as her mind. I put my man in his
class and my woman in hers, and I arranged them in a pattern
which allowed me to show: first, the man in his world, with her
comment upon it; second, the pair of them together; third, the woman
in her world, with his comment upon it; and last, the pair of them
forever separate. ("Preface," p. ix)

The method, as Howard explains, was intended to create a
better sense of reality. Simplicity of characterization alone,
however, is more likely to weaken the entire dramatic structure; the principals become cardboard supports. After a while
we don't believe in them. "Those who misunderstood," Howard
writes, "found nothing in it [the play] to enjoy—neither plot,
idea, hero, nor heroine" ("Preface," p. xi). And the fault, to

be honest, was not because the audience was ill prepared for this kind of rather depressing realism; the fault, ironically, was in the playwright forgetting to do what he usually does best— present exciting theater, even melodramatic at times if necessary. It seems Howard has a noble conception here, evidently carefully thought out; but he is somehow never able to do enough with it. A story of the lady and the gangster is a popular choice for the 1920's—particularly with the great style and imagination of Scott Fitzgerald to evoke a kind of poetry; or with the comic abilities of Damon Runyon. Lacking these, however, Howard is a little out of his depth. The result is a construction not a creation.

True, the play does hold some interesting views of the author. For example, the following excerpt from the Preface on love is very informative—but doesn't really justify the static character of the principals: "And finally, I refused to allow their deep love for one another to help them in the slightest degree, because whatever dramatists and novelists may write to mislead young people into romance, love remains the only thing which fails humanity more treacherously than religion does" ("Preface," p. xi). The deep love of the McCarvers is never convincing, at least never convincing in the only way that counts in the dramatic vein—theatrically. It is this fact alone which is so striking about *Lucky Sam McCarver* that a playwright so adept at good theatricality would believe that he could give it all up in this particular play and try to rely on a concept alone to hold an audience. All good plays depend on tricks, conventional arrangements which we willingly accept, which make the reality that much more real. This is theatricalism at its best, what makes the dramatized piece speak so convincingly for life. Howard's concept for Sam and Carlotta is an intriguing one—"there seemed to be nothing that either one could say or do or desire or believe that did not outrage the other" ("Preface," p. xii)—but translating that into theater is a greater challenge than he realized.

Essentially, Carlotta is another Daisy Buchanan, the heroine of *The Great Gatsby*. She represents the young, idle, rich women of the 1920's who fascinated both writers. Howard describes Carlotta: "There is nothing tangibly wrong with her and yet she is, in some curious and intangible way, a little tarnished."

The comparisons with Fitzgerald's masterpiece are interesting. Both women are involved with murders; both men (Gatsby and Sam) are somewhat involved in shielding them. The same basic irony exists, that the two lords of the underworld eventually appear less corrupt than the careless "innocents" they protect.

II　Ned McCobb's Daughter *(1926)*

1926 was a banner year for Howard with two successes running at the same time on Broadway. *Ned McCobb's Daughter* and *The Silver Cord,* both Theatre Guild productions, ran in repertory with Shaw's *Pygmalion* in two houses.[6] Popularity was fairly well guaranteed by the use of underworld principals involved with bootlegging. Compared to the previous year's failure, *Lucky Sam McCarver,* also about the underworld, *Ned McCobb's Daughter* had the fortunate advantage of a very likeable heroine, Carrie, completely in the mold of the plucky Amy in *They Knew What They Wanted.* Evidently, Howard had learned his lesson well in 1925 and was now content to use the simpler theatrical devices that had worked before. This time the setting is a small restaurant ("Carrie's Spa") at a ferry crossing of the Kennebec River in Maine. Captain McCobb, the proud but taciturn old Yankee, runs the ferry with his son-in-law George Callahan. Carrie Callahan runs the restaurant. She is very much her father's daughter: "She never gives the impression of hurry and she is never idle. She realizes, without ever having given the matter a thought, that she is the equal of any man. She has had a hard time, few ups and many, many downs, but her disasters have left her unscarred. She wants all that she can possibly get materially, but she is unconscious of lacking anything mentally or spiritually."

The plot involves the prospect of a new bridge which will put Captain McCobb out of business. Characteristically, the resourceful Carrie sees progress another way: a new bridge means more travellers and maybe more customers at the spa. She wants to expand and to add a new kitchen. As in *Lucky Sam McCarver,* Prohibition comes in for more stage ridicule. Local Federal men bring confiscated rum ("real Santa Cruz rum") to Carrie as a gift. George's brother Babe arrives at the spa, identity unknown to the others. The mysterious stranger is an old theatrical device which Howard uses numerous times. Although it can become a cheap melodramatic suspense point when used to excess, the device is still effective if used moderately. The Federal men, however, recognize him as someone wanted for bootlegging. When finally introduced as George's brother, Babe reveals their history. Ten years earlier they had left New York City, Babe to the South and George to Boston. George in time met Carrie, a nurse. Trouble with the law put George in jail for one year; actually the confinement would have been longer without Carrie's basic honesty. She suggested pleading guilty: "I always think it's better jest t' out and say you done wrong, if you hev."

The plot moves into higher gear with George being accused of stealing $2000 of the ferry fares. He is confronted by Carrie's brother, Ben, a police officer, and the lawyer, Grover. Shocked as he is, Captain McCobb (and the company) agrees to accept George's resignation if the money is returned by the next day. Carrie accepts this additional burden, saying that somehow she'll get the money. Of course, all of this is to establish the quality of Carrie's personal courage and basic honesty. The rather simple, trusting nature of *all* the McCobbs is demonstrated by the Captain's strange story of how he was once swindled out of $175,000 in a business venture and did nothing about it. The Captain turns the experience into a maxim: "Seems like lookin' after the weak must be the price a real man has t'pay fer bein' able t' look after himself. Don't guess it's no different fer a real woman, Carrie." Although we might well argue the merit of the Captain's tolerance, the story serves well enough to place the audience's sympathy with the McCobbs, father and daughter. Stories of the unregenerate husband seem rather conventional during the 1920's. Howard had used the theme earlier in his story of Mrs. Vietch and the husband who deserted her with an infant child. Certainly, with statistical evidence to support the real facts, the audience's familiarity with the problem made it a powerful, sentimental situation for popular theater. The curtain falls as the Captain suffers a fatal stroke—just as he is about to reveal the reason George borrowed a thousand dollars the previous year. The Captain is determined, before Carrie, to establish George's real, infamous character. Death upholds the suspense.

A. *The Unsinkable Carrie McCobb*

The second and third acts are set in the McCobb's parlor where the Captain is laid out. A bit morbid for today's taste, the last two acts are played in the "presence" of the Captain's remains. Our introduction to the waitress, Jenny, provides some suspicion of a liaison with George. Her "recital" of her hard life sounds familiar in the growing chain of Howard's downtrodden women. Meanwhile, and always in the background, is the person of the enigmatic Babe who either directly or by implication has some cynical comment about these people's lives. The gangster personality of Babe is, frankly, better established by a good actor (as Alfred Lunt was to do) than by anything particularly revealing in his few lines. While Carrie agonizes over her financial difficulties—more so now that her father is gone—, Babe remains as a kind of watchful witness. In one of his few statements, he voices praise for her character: "... dat's what counts in dis world. Character. By God, if it don't! Beauty fades, but character goes on forever. You know. Huh? I don't know nothin' I admire like I do character. Dat's George's trouble. He ain't got none."

Babe tells Carrie that they two are alike and that a business deal he has in mind will help them both. In a major confrontation scene with her erring husband, Carrie gives what is almost a credo for the loyal, long-suffering wives she represents: "I ain't accusin' you of nuthin'! You're my husband. I married you for better or worse and you ain't been so bad you couldn't hev been worse. You ain't been a drinkin' man and you ain't never hurt me. You've given me plenty t' regret, but you ain't never made me mad. Guess that's more'n most women kin say 'bout their husbands. I jest hev t' remember that. You ain't strong like I am and you don't think twice like I do. Well, so long as you don't make me mad. . . ." This is a remarkable speech. The language is crisp, to the point, and very convincing in establishing Carrie's character; it is one of the best examples of Howard's excellent ear for local speech. What is even more striking is the way the lines reveal the complexity of the unregenerate husband. True, Carrie in her homespun brand of rationalizing has reduced much to an almost amusing simplicity, but the complex network still remains for the audience to mull over. This is the essence of excellent social satire: we have the muddled human response and the essential predicament at the same time. How revealing all this is of social affairs fifty and more years ago. Notice how basically moral Carrie's attitude ("fer better or worse") is; the possibility of divorce seems completely remote. How little she expects of the marriage, how thankful she is for not having for a husband an alcoholic or a wife-beater. The lines read like a social document.

George replies, "I'd think I done enough t'make God Almighty mad." Carrie answers. "I ain't God Almighty." And, of course, here's the crux of the matter (and the appeal of the story): she is only herself, which is enough, and she is there not to dispense justice or anything like that; she is the brave woman of the times (a kind of "indomitable Molly") who will simply do the best she can. Popular sentiment is served; melodrama awaits. Characteristic of Howard, Carrie is so much her own woman that not even religion can help. When Grover offers to console her with appropriate lines from the Bible she shocks him by preferring the amusing passages instead. "Guess mebbe you better not read t'me," she says to him "Never could keep my mind on religion when I hed anythin' important t'think 'bout." There will be more things to think about quite soon as the plot begins to quicken and Babe abruptly becomes the center of the developing melodrama. Alone with George, Babe forces a suspected truth out of him, that the Captain had mortgaged the house for a thousand dollars to help Jenny who was to have George's child. Babe gives his conditions: Carrie and Babe will become business partners and the house (and George) will in a way be hostages. Babe will pay their debts if he can store his bootleg liquor here and run his business from the spa. Carrie reluctantly agrees but also reminds them that her fires are merely banked for the moment: "You two are brothers jest the same as Pa an' me's father and daughter. You're two of a kind and Pa and me's two of a kind. Your pair's got the pair of us licked. I got one thing over Pa, though. Pa's dead of his lickin' but I ain't dead of mine! Not by a long sight, I ain't!"

In the third act, the following morning, events continue to build up: George gets the wild idea of taking some of their new funds and running off with Jenny. He says he has had enough of righteous Yankees. However, the plan fails as Babe takes a firmer control of things. He even relates the entire involvement of George and Jenny to the astonished Carrie who somehow never guessed. In a major scene between Carrie and Babe the elements of traditional melodrama begin steadily to mount up. With the intent of getting things as black as possible for Carrie ("before the dawn"), Babe announces his plans to have Carrie's children give the spa a respectable appearance while the bootleggers move in. When Carrie fights this idea and wants to send the children away, Babe counters by threatening to turn in George and somehow implicate Carrie so that they would both be jailed. Then he would make himself, as the brother, the children's guardian and still have his way. Preposterous as all this sounds (what about Carrie's brother, Ben, the police officer?) it serves to galvanize our heroine into action. Extreme tolerance for a worthless husband is one thing, but Motherhood is another matter entirely. As Howard describes her frantic position, she is "terrified but still thinking."

Full of fight now, the redoubtable Carrie cooks up a plan to defeat Babe. To the admiring Babe she pretends to go along with the scheme (he likes her spunk), even convinces him to give her another thousand to do the kitchen, and then shouts for the Federal men in the spa to apprehend Babe. Although the authorities are not really present, the ruse works and Babe runs off with George. Carrie—and the forces of right—have won! It should be stressed immediately that it is the nature of melodrama to work events quickly and sensationally so that the audience never has time to ask unanswerable questions of cause and effect. Otherwise, as in the reading of the play, we can see a number of inconsistencies in Carrie's great plan to overcome Babe. Sufficient, on stage, that the resourceful Carrie has carried the day: to the amazed Ben, Jenny, and the others (including the mute coffin) she throws off the last lines of the play: "I know I ought to be cryin', but I can't help laughin'. [*To her dead father.*] Excuse me, Pa!"

Generally, the play was well received; three of eleven daily

New York reviewers included it in their ten best plays of the
1926–27 season. Robert Coleman, however, thought it was a
grim, ironic comedy of death.[7] Charles Brackett thought the
last act was an entertainment alone, and bad literature.[8] Major
drama critics, such as Joseph Wood Krutch and John Mason
Brown, taking the long view for American dramatic literature,
deplored the excessive melodrama. Although Krutch praised the
theme and the excellent characterizations, he complained that
the play "steadily degenerates as it goes along, because at
every turn the author takes the easiest way, and ends in sheer
melodrama."[9] Brown, with O'Neill very much on the mind
(*Beyond the Horizon,* 1920), spoke up for the good use of
native materials and realistic dialect, the "pungency and honesty" of the characters. However, he wrote that Howard
seemed more concerned with making a "show" than a play.
The play has "stretches of such good and salty writing that it
is doubly exasperating to find that all of its realism is but the
preamble to some foolish fairy tale."[10] By a "show," of course,
he meant that it was an excellent vehicle for good actors, an
opinion with which most critics generally agreed. There was a
rather universal agreement that Howard and O'Neill together
were opening up necessary new ground in realistic American
theatre. According to Glenn Hughes, "Only Eugene O'Neill has
surpassed Howard in the delineation of such American types as
bootleggers, sea-captains, nightclub operators, and hardbitten
but noble women."[11]

III The Silver Cord *(1926)*

Appropriateness is never a bad quality when applied to Broadway stage successes. Certainly, the popularity of *The Silver
Cord* is another reminder that a subject of the times—a contest
between traditional and modern womanhood—will always have
its audience. Equally fortunate is Sidney Howard's bold decision
to fashion his play around the extreme possessiveness of a
dominant mother, which in some ways may even be a universal
subject. The further advantage for the 1920's is the intriguing
novelty of a Freudian interpretation. With O'Neill darkly
leading the way, contemporary audiences were becoming fa-

miliar with the signs and formulae of subconscious desires. The basic plot of *The Silver Cord* is simple enough: Mrs Phelps, long widowed from a loveless marriage, is determined to run her sons' lives despite the natural "encroachments" of their women.

The story takes place in a fashionable residential area in the East. David, the older son, has brought home his bride of a few months, Christina, for a visit. Robert, the other son, has his fiancée, Hester, to introduce. A reasonable amount of tension exists considering the sons' longstanding dependence on their mother, Mrs. Phelps. As expected, Mrs. Phelps can hardly restrain herself since she hasn't seen David during the two years he's been in Europe. Christina is nearly ignored in the excitement. Even at this early point there is no doubt that the neglect is not accidental. Almost as a shock, the couple find that the mother has placed them in separate rooms—David in his old room next to Mrs. Phelps. What, of course, becomes immediately central to the plot is the almost total inability of Mrs. Phelps to understand someone like Christina.

Christina, one of Howard's major portraits, is a completely modern woman. Howard describes her as "intelligent, trusting, courageous." Of course, the fact that she is a biologist—a doctor in fact—is incomprehensible to Mrs. Phelps; the distinction is made early by the mother between Christina and a "real doctor." When Mrs. Phelps learns that Christina has a post waiting for her in New York with the Rockefeller Institute, she counters with a fantastic suggestion for keeping the couple with her. She describes the opportunities of the local clinic: "We've just got in a new microscope, too. Oh, a very fine one! One the High School didn't want any more. You'll simply love our laboratory. Oh, you will! It has a splendid new sink with hot and cold running water and quite a good gas stove because it's also the nurses' washroom and diet kitchen. And you'll be allowed to putter around as much as you like whenever it isn't in use by the nurses or the real doctors."

Christina remains polite but adamant. Quietly insistent, she tries to educate the parochial Mrs. Phelps to the modern world. In a good reply to the mother's boast that "David always had my ideas and they're very sound ones," Christina counters with "perhaps they aren't sound for David." The notion that David

should work his own way up, be a small frog in a large ocean
(New York), makes little sense to Mrs. Phelps. The scene ends
with the adversary relation clearly drawn between the two. However, before it does, Mrs. Phelps does give a somewhat sentimental and ringing defense of motherhood: "Give us our due,
Christina. We weren't entirely bustles and smelling salts, we
girls who did not go into the world. We made a great profession
which I fear may be in some danger of vanishing from the face
of the earth. We made a profession of motherhood." The impasse
continues.

Robert's affairs seem equally precarious. The combination of
mother's assertiveness and his characteristic hesitancy has him
thoroughly confused. Slight as it is—the matter of Hester's *calm*
preparation for marriage—the question becomes portentous to
Robert. Perhaps, she doesn't care enough for him? A little
prodding here and there and finally Robert promises his mother
he'll break off the engagement. A good indication of how things
are between them, the degree of control the mother exercises,
is Robert's willingness to lay his head in her lap and talk "in
the old way." For a twenty-six year old young man it is a
remarkable posture. Some Freudian inspired guesswork seems
in order here despite Howard's contention that none exists in
the play. The Theatre Guild directors insisted on discussing the
play along these lines despite Howard's stated objections to any
intellectual formulae.[13] The audience, quite obviously, needed
little persuasion to see the mother-son relationship as increasingly
unhealthy.

Circumstances tighten as we learn that Christina is five months
pregnant. The fact seems to increase Mrs. Phelps' hostility
toward her—and toward Hester who continually speaks up for
her. Although younger by ten years (only twenty), Hester is cut
of the same mold as Christina. They are two exceedingly
modern young ladies who intend to fight for their men. "You
just leave things to me," Hester counsels the uncertain Robert.
"If we're poor, I'll cook and scrub floors. I'll bring up our
children. I'll take care of you whether we live in New York or
Kamchatka." Nevertheless, in a highly melodramatic confrontation scene, she forces the truth out of him: that he really wants
to break the engagement. She knows this is his mother's doing,

she returns his ring, and becomes nearly hysterical. Incredibly, while others try to calm Hester, the mother voices concern over Robert's nerves. The scene ends on a high pitch as Hester is determined to leave the house tonight. When she tries to call a cab (against Mrs. Phelps' wishes), the mother rips the telephone from the wall.

A. Mothers and Sons

There is a necessary interval before the next scene to allow the setting to be changed to David's bedroom. Mrs. Phelps fusses about the room, preparing it for the night, picking up clothes, spreading a comforter. Rather hard to accept are the stage directions for her to bestow "devout maternal kisses and hugs" on the clothes—and even the pillow. When David returns ready for bed he is not entirely happy to have his mother waiting for him. Mrs. Phelps recalls the old days when this was a familiar routine, when they talked late at night, in a kind of "imaginary kingdom where we were king and queen." The issue returns to the now familiar one of the "unnatural" separation of mothers and sons. She blames the scientific age for breaking the strongest bond on earth. Scenes of this order give some credence to Arthur Hornblow's contention that the play is basically "more a debate than a drama," and at its worst, "one long lecture divided into parts."[14] Nevertheless, certain facts and feelings must be brought out into the open between mother and son. Later when the "debate" continues in the room with both sons present, we realize to what extent Robert is tied to his mother—the umbilical "silver cord." Against David's accusations, he defends the need to break the engagement with Hester: she wasn't up to the ideal of womanhood that their mother represented.

Finally, after many comings and goings, Christina is alone with David in his bedroom to say goodnight—her own room being down the hall and Mrs. Phelps conveniently in the adjacent room. (They all know that every word can be overheard.) What follows is the obligatory full confrontation we have been waiting for. David attempts to allay Christina's fears, tries to make the case for his mother's hard, self-sacrificing life, facts which

Christina cynically rejects. The structure of the discussion is clever to an extent since she continually draws him out to say the things about the mother-son relationship which are obviously at the core of the problem. However, David doesn't seem to realize the inherent dangers. Scientist that she is, Christina calmly puts things together for herself—and the audience. A further and necessary point is the effect of the mother on David's basic personality; he has a tendency at times to retire entirely into himself, leaving Christina adrift, cut off. "It's your mother's land," she tells him, "arid, sterile, and your mother's! You won't let me get in there. Worse than that, you won't let life get in there! Or she won't!"

Almost on cue, Mrs. Phelps reenters from the near doorway. Obviously, she has heard everything. Christina leaves the field momentarily to mother and son. A rather standard mother-martyr speech follows which puts David weakly back into the maternal fold. In all, fairly unbelievable dialogue: Mother, "I've still got my big boy, after all?" David replies, "You bet you've got him."

The act ends with the kind of melodramatic commotion which most critics recognize as the standard Ibsenite device to halt endless discussions.[15] Screams resound through the house, windows are flung open—we had already been told about treacherous holes in the ice pond—and all attention is given to the plight of the distraught Hester who has run out toward the pond and the road. As the boys fly out of the house to the rescue, Mrs. Phelps, single minded as ever, calls after them in a frenzy to return and get their coats.

The essential purpose in the final act is to provide a platform for Christina, that is, almost literally a commanding level from which she can lecture Mrs. Phelps on proper womanhood and motherhood. Hester, of course, remains upstairs, recovering from her hysterics; the other principals gather in the living room to straighten out the dilemma of last evening. In a nearly blunt, but certainly forceful way, Christina takes command, even insisting that the mother stay for the discussion or else lose David entirely. Christina accuses her of being unfit "to be anyone's mother," gives details on her errors in child raising. The tone is very detached, scientific, similar to a trial lawyer; Howard describes her as "Joan of Arc raising the siege of Orleans." The full pronouncements on *proper* motherhood are major statements for the play, rich with sentimental appeal and ringing conviction. Capping a long series of "contributions" she vows to give her husband, she shocks Mrs. Phelps with the final item: "and the enjoyment of my body. To which I have reason to believe he is not indifferent."[16]

Mrs. Phelps' defense becomes for her the major speech of the play: she gives the long history of her loveless marriage to an older man (which, seemingly, explains much) and how love for the boys became the romance of her life. The issue now is clearly drawn: David must choose since Christina is determined to leave with Hester. Frantically, he decides to run after them, now apparently trapped into making a decision. The final scene is a pathetic replaying of the bedroom scene with Robert kneeling in the arms of his mother. She still has, she reminds him, "one of my great sons." In a voice which grows stronger and more convincing—and then possibly unsure—she closes the play, using some lines from the Bible: "And you must remember that David, in his blindness, has forgotten. That mother love suffereth long and is kind; envieth not, is not puffed up, is not easily provoked; beareth all things; believeth all things; hopeth all things; endureth all things. . . . At least, I think *my* love does?" Robert, now "engulfed forever," answers weakly: "Yes, Mother."

B. *A Little Freud*

The majority of Howard's plays are based on character, with enough variety of strong types to fashion an interesting story. Certainly, he has never approached playwriting from the view of the intellectual in the theater. He is more at home with rather simple, straightforward issues. It is helpful to recall some of these basic qualities of Howard as a playwright in considering *The Silver Cord,* which ironically is the only rationalistic formula play he wrote. The rationalistic formula consists of the Freudian principles—whether publicly admitted by Howard or not. The audience, quite properly, is fascinated by the unmasking of Mrs. Phelps, the professional mother; the Oedipus complex stares us boldly in the face with the love she holds for her sons. What comes to mind are the nagging thoughts that such involvements are potentially explosive stage materials. The question might be asked: Is it possible to use only a little of Freud? I suppose, in all honesty, we would have to answer, Yes, since bits of Freud are everywhere in modern life. It might then be a rather skillful accomplishment for Howard to have used what he wanted of Freud on the most obvious popular level and not to have gone beyond his own safe water limits. More foolhardy writers have been known to play out of their depth, using theatrical devices to suggest what may be basically unclear, vague—or even false.

Stark Young sensed some of these difficulties when he said that Mrs. Phelps had to be interpreted as either "fairly absurd or as a diseased and ominous figure." The latter would demand a more complex and darker tone, implying "a far deeper talent than Mr. Howard possesses." What results is the first possibility: the mother becomes "slightly farcical." The basic superficiality of her character becomes obvious; she is portrayed as "bold without power and humility about the great forces of life."[17] Fortunately, Howard had the talented Laura Hope Crews to interpret the part. Contemporary reviews uniformly praise her clever handling of a difficult part; she put much wit into the role and read the mother as an absurd exaggeration.

The London critic, Desmond McCarthy, viewing the British production with Lillian Braithwaite as Mrs. Phelps, felt the play was too much like a chess game in which "the free spirit of life is apt to evaporate." His fundamental brief was against deductive art in which some general proposition controls a particular case. McCarthy considered the new Freudian psychology a clever way to expand human nature "in a manner apparently profound." Characters under this method were "no longer born but made up according to psychological prescriptions."[18] Nevertheless, other London critics admired the play for its careful construction and analytical quality. The play marked the first appearance of Clare Eames in London. Playing the part of Christina, she had already earned a fair reputation as a major actress.

The character of Christina we recognize as another strong-minded Howard woman. Compared to previous heroines, such as

Amy in *They Knew What They Wanted* and Carrie in *Ned McCobb's Daughter,* she is the only one equipped professionally as well as emotionally to order her own life. Critics thought it an ingenious device to make her a biologist, "full of explanations and of informations that put people in their places."[19] The characterization seems to be a completely believable one. What does test the credulity at times is the rather doltish behavior of the sons. But here again our acceptance would have to depend on how we view the mother; to what extent are we willing to grant her the mesmeric power she seems to hold over her sons? In a letter to his sister in 1926 Howard said that the story was based on Clare's family (others have said the source was Howard's own family) and that it was a "wicked, humorous tirade" against mothers. "It is a story," he said, "worth telling in a Rotarian world."[20]

IV Half Gods *(1929)*

It is always of interest when a play depends on a close, autobiographic reference. Difficulties with his wife, Clare, had begun early in 1928: by the fall they were formally separated and for the next two years Howard, despondent, lived in his sister's home in Berkeley. *Half Gods,* then, is a rather curious attempt by Howard to appraise marriage and divorce, and perhaps, say some pertinent things about the difficulties of being really "modern."[21] The dismal failure of the play proved the truth of Krutch's remarks that you can't write out of personal irritation alone, even if it be moral indignation.[22]

The play, set in New York City, is structured in nine scenes, hopefully fast moving as in a film: "one scene can fade into the next," are the instructions. The principals are Stephen, lawyer, Harvard graduate; and Hope, his wife. They have two small children. Their good friend, Rush, after two marriages, is the bachelor cynic and man about town. Hope's older sister, Helena, divorced ten years, completes the foursome. At the very outset of the action, the attempt is made to present spritely, modern young people, a bit confused at times but, nevertheless, more comic than tragic. In their fashionable apartment Stephen and Hope are having their troubles: Hope keeps him out too late

at night, Stephen demands more sleep. Hope even forgets to
pay the gas bill. Stephen gives indications of coming to some
major decision about marriage: "All you young wives! Do you
know what your husbands are saying about you? That you're
not worth the price! That's what! Not worth the price!" By the
second scene, it is Hope, however, who has left him. She leaves
for the Plaza with the children. Consoled by Rush and Judge
Sturgis, of Stephen's law firm, the abandoned husband gets
conflicting advice. Rush suggests a new woman for him (from
his "stud book") and a trip to Reno for a divorce. The Judge,
as expected, counsels patience and defends marriage.

As the Judge leaves, Helena and Hope enter. Not always
apparent, however, is the real distinction that Helena is supposed
to have. Evidently, Howard had high hopes for another major
female characterization; she is described as a woman of "high
standards and considerable worldly intelligence." Quite likely,
the problem with the characterization is the continual failure
of intended devastating, clever final lines. (Here again, a
Behrman or Barry is wanted.) Helena's solution, to some extent,
is to offer Hope a job in her bookstore. Let Hope have the
opportunity to test her freedom, let her "get rid of her delusions,"
she counsels. Hope follows with what is supposed to be a somewhat passionate yet comic speech on her need to be wanted.
"I've even thought: if only he'd get pneumonia and nearly die!
I did have one hopeful moment when you were threatened with
appendicitis! But you cured that with your lemon juice. [Estab-
lished early is the running gag of Stephen's universal reliance
on lemon juice.] You did for our marriage with your damn
lemon juice, Steve!" The scene ends with Hope's determination
to stay apart.

The next scene provides some topical humor with Hope's
visit to the Freudian psychiatrist, Dr. Mannering. It is obvious
that the stress on the new Freudian terms (ego-conscious, anima,
libido) was designed for comic effects, which, of course, by
now are somewhat dulled. Nevertheless, there is still some
effective satire. Stephen also turns up in the doctor's office, and
tries to evade being another subject for analysis. Somehow,
Hope agrees to return home as a free woman. Things move along
under the new arrangement, but with Stephen's rising suspicions

that Hope spends too much time with Rush in the bookstore. There is a partly amusing scene in which Hope teases Rush into going away with her. Evidently the charade, which frightens Rush away, is to demonstrate how really modern and free she now is. Helena bumbles into the rather confusing scene and condemns them all for being unfaithful to marriage. She champions men against the revolt of women, giving some very effective lines on the subject: "I'm fed to the teeth on the penny dreadful bolshevism you young things go in for these days! Fidelity not important! Other people's feelings not important! Let me tell you, my dear sister, you need self-discipline a lot more than you need self-expression!"

Scene Five, almost a mandatory scene in attempts at sophisticated comedy, has the principals in the police station the next morning in a small Long Island town. It seems Stephen is charged with drunk driving following a fight with Rush the night before. Hope and Judge Sturgis are there to "rescue" him. Things with the law are literally "fixed," and reconciliation seems in the wings for the couple when we belatedly learn that there was a girl, Pauline, with him. The on-again-off-again melodrama continues and they separate again. Months later, they meet in the Judge's office to talk divorce. Hope shocks everyone by saying she'll give the children to Stephen and *she'll* visit. She admits they "drive me mad!" She launches into a major speech on her freedoms—to live as she pleases, love when she pleases, and generally keep her duty to herself as her first consideration. Interesting as all these startling (and dramatic) views are, they fail to convince us since they lack substance in Hope's characterization. The triflings that have happened so far on the stage fail to support such bold convictions. One has the feeling that the personally involved Howard has things of his own to get off his chest and rather arbitrarily moves things around. Not by any means arbitrary is the very provocative way Howard chooses to introduce the title. Dismayed with what he has heard from the young couple, the Judge admonishes them by reading the last stanza from Emerson's "Give All to Love."

> "Though thou loved her as thyself,
> As a self of purer clay,

Though her parting dims the day,
Stealing grace from all alive;
Heartily know,
When half-gods go,
The gods arrive."

Actually, the poem is a rather strange reconciliation to marriage since it holds Emerson's Platonic views that succeeding love ("the gods arrive") might be superior to the existing one ("half-gods"). Or at the least, as one could surmise, we are led to be realistic about the present and perhaps not tempt providence either way.

A. *"Keystone Comedy"*

Scene Seven, what Howard called his "Keystone Comedy" scene, is a bold but ineffective attempt to do broad comedy. We are in the apartment and everyone is running and moving about in conflicting directions; the hapless porters are unsure as to whose trunks go up and whose go down the stairs. Hope is leaving for Reno. The kids have the whooping cough, Stephen has a cold—and his lemon juice. In the "mad" scene that follows, a comic Dr. Wohlheim gives the parents a lecture on the responsibility to children, as basic biology demands. No man, he concludes, should put assunder "the breeders of the healthy young." Still unsure who's staying and who's leaving, Stephen gives confusing orders to the porters on the stairs. As we might guess by now, the porters drop the trunks. Things come to an incredulous halt when Hope slaps Stephen on the face—and he hits her with a left hook, knocking her out! The porter, professional-like, counts her out. This scene, which Howard admitted to Barrett Clark "was the only thing I was sure of in the play," was worked over very carefully. He also admits in the same letter that nearly everyone kept "telling me how lousy that scene is" (Clark, p. 209).

The next day arrangements are made by the estranged couple with private detectives at Stephen's apartment; they are to stage a liaison with Pauline for a divorce action by adultery. (Whatever happened to Reno?) Hope telephones and comes up with Rush, and once more we have the on-again-off-again attachment of Stephen and Hope. This time she wants him. (Perhaps the knockout straightened her out.) They leave. Rush and Pauline kiss and make up in the apartment as the detectives come rushing in to "verify" the adultery with the wrong parties. Another big confusion scene of doubtful comic value follows. In the final scene, the same evening, the couple are completely reconciled to themselves—and marriage. Hope even admits that maybe she needed the blow on the chin. She wants marriage now. Life has left them two people alone who need to be together: "We're not big enough to be out alone!" Hope makes a major speech, defending her new views: "I had ideas! I've got over 'em! I thought I had great wasted powers in me! I haven't! I wanted a place in the outside world! My place there's worth about two cents! I was bored with all this! I've only just seen all this for the first time! ... I thought there was more romance in life for me! That turned out the silliest mess of all!" Even though Stephen still has doubts how it will work out, he finally agrees. "Why should I," he concludes, "be afraid of unhappiness?"

In many ways the play is a very curious piece. Although there are a number of good opportunities for a full development of the characters and the plot's cause and effect, Howard seems almost perversely to take the easiest route and to give us trifles instead. Not that we would mind the trifles in themselves—they can well support a proper light comedy—but in this play Howard is aiming for some major considerations, and he does insist on articulating these views through his characters even though they completely lack conviction. For example, the last speech of Hope has great possibilities. It is the reverse of the usual position of the new liberated woman: here, Hope finds she's not up to all the freedom; there is no "own thing" that she can do. All of great interest—except it fails theatrically because none of these new realizations has been dramatized.

"A dull, heavy polemic on marriage," a contemporary reviewer wrote. What a travesty of Howard's talents was the general complaint. The review continues: "a complete lack of control, an hysterical wandering between invective and burlesque that were both equally outside his theme. ... So intent, apparently, was Mr. Howard on adapting his theme to a predetermined form that the result left his characters a set of brittle, rasping puppets, moving nowhere with feverish futility."[23]

CHAPTER 5

Plays of the 1930's ...
Bean ... Dodsworth

I Lute Song (1930)

SIDNEY Howard's interest in what was to become *Lute Song* dates from around 1925.[1] After World War I, his fellow adapter, Will Irwin, found a copy of a French translation of the ancient Chinese classic and showed it to Howard.[2] The original play, *Pi-Pa-Ki* was written by Kao-Tong-Kia in ancient China, and adapted by Mao-Taou in 1404 for presentation at the Imperial Court of Peking. It has enjoyed, Howard points out, a continuous stage life since that time. The play is a classic on the Chinese stage as *Hamlet* is on ours.

It it difficult to say why Howard began the collaboration with Irwin. Considering the recent success of *They Knew What They Wanted,* it may well be that he was flushed enough with new confidence to take on readily a number of theater possibilities. During these years the record shows that he was also preparing three translations, the pageant *Lexington,* and *Lucky Sam McCarver.* Enough for any playwright. Perhaps, the interest in the Chinese play derived from the challenge to compose somewhat in the bare clipped manner of the Orient and to adopt some of the conventions of the Chinese stage. Simplicity, of course, is the keynote throughout. A raised platform serves for all the scenes—the house of Tsai in the country or later, the Pavillion of the Palace of Prince Nieou, as well as all other places. To indicate the changes different types of hangings of various colors are used. No properties are used; all rests in the imagination, except for a table.

In the Prologue, the manager enters, bows, and speaks before the curtain. In lyrical terms he talks of the venerable tale of

the past, "when gods walked upon earth." In a rather charming
way he readies the audience: "Do not be afraid—we shall
leave nothing out, and we hope to be finished before morning."
The first scene takes place at the House of Tsai, the simple
country home of Tsai-Yong the student; his wife, Tchao-Ou-
Niang; and his parents, Tsai and Mme. Tsai. Tsai-Yong talks
earnestly with Tschang (who also takes the part of the Manager) about the seriousness of his studies. "The Fourth Maxim,"
he says, is "so profound that we are commanded not to understand it." Tschang, the family counselor, urges the young man
to go to the capital and be examined. The matter of self-
advancement now becomes the issue as the parents join the
discussion. Tsai-Yong seems reluctant to use his wisdom for
personal gain, and is concerned about the welfare of his elderly
parents when he is gone.

The exchanges here, extremely formal and ritualistic for the
most part, present the heart of the old play. What are the
responsibilities of a son to his parents? To what use are
studies if not for advancement? The father, who urges him to
leave, talks of the pride they will have in his fame. Even
though the wife has vowed to care for the parents, the mother
agrees with her son and cautions them on a possibly wrong
decision. She tells a parable of the perils to come if the son
leaves home. The debate ends, however, with Tsai commanding
his son to leave for the capital.

The next scene is at the Pavillion of the Palace of Prince Nieou.
The Prince admonishes his daughter, the Princess Nieou-Chi, for
not cooperating with him in his attempts to find her a husband.
It is important for his "intellectual reputation" that he be able
to run his home properly. The Emperor, however, has found the
man; it is announced that she will marry the new Chief Magistrate. We are not particularly surprised to learn that, lo and
behold, the Magistrate is our Tsai-Yong! He is the young scholar
the servants were gossiping about at the beginning of the scene.
Evidently, the promises of his success have been fulfilled. The
scene ends with the "astonishment" of his announced name. The
pattern of all the successive scenes throughout the three acts is
a shifting back and forth from the parents' house to the Palace.
Some of these are quite short, merely sufficient to show the con-

ditions in each place. When we see the parents' home again, we see that the mother's prophecy of the future is coming about. They are extremely poor, their rice field is gone, and the daughter has sold her bridal clothes and her jewels. The mother berates the father for letting Tsai-Yong go. The father takes it all philosophically—"To all men, sooner or later, misfortune comes."

At the Emperor's Palace, what is call the Palace of the Voice of Jade, the young magistrate's problems begin in earnest. He refuses to marry the Princess, announces he is married and must return to the provinces to help his parents. Nevertheless, the authorities insist that he do as they wish. He must forget the past and "pay the price of greatness." The soldiers surround him and the wedding is arranged. The beautiful Princess Nieou-Chi complains on her wedding night that she "loves a shadow"; the distraught bridegroom has left her, seeking, as he says, his old lute to play the love tune she requests. The scene shifts to the Provincial Granary where the loyal wife, Tchao-Ou-Niang, waits in line for the charity rice. It is a nightmarish moment as the respectable looking woman is attacked by a horde of beggars and loses the rice. She believes she has failed her husband "even as a beggar."

A. *The Dutiful Wife*

Tsai-Yong attempts to send money to his parents but it is intercepted by the Prince who maintains that "the past is the past." The entrapment deepens. At the House of Tsai conditions have reached their lowest point. They are in a state of famine; the mother becomes quarrelsome and distrusts the best intentions of the dutiful wife. Tsai sees it as a heaven sent calamity "to prove to us the goodness of our son's wife." The mother forgives her and dies, and soon after, the father also dies. The loyal wife vows that somehow she will arrange a proper burial for them. This she accomplishes by selling her hair. At the burial place, the holy man tells her that she must go to the Palace in the dress of a novice and find her husband. She will tell him of the death of his parents so that he can perform the required rites. And to earn her way for the journey she will play the lute, the lost lute of Tsai-Yong which the holy man gives her. The nature

of these events seems to be the equivalent of some divine order
in her life. We are informed by the Manager in the Prologue
to the final act that the wife is exceptional (as all women are),
and that like the willow she has the quality of a lasting strength.

At the Palace we find the strange new situation of the sympathetic Princess offering to help Tsai-Yong in his predicament.
Characteristic of Howard's usual strong women characters, the
Princess is determined to help once she knows all the circumstances. She speaks in figures: "When the world's wickedness
bears its bitter fruit, it is women that must harvest it!" However,
the Prince will only allow the parents and wife to be sent for.
He would not agree to a journey to the provinces. The wife, by
this time, has arrived at the Temple in the capital city. In a
rather predictable, ironic way she recognizes her husband although he fails to know the poor novice with the lute. She has
a stranger give him the lute with the brief message, "They
wait no more."

The final scene is the resolution in which somehow everything
is known to everyone and all the wrongs are carefully righted.
Suitable to the necessary sense of the marvelous, the wife by
accident comes to the Princess and tells her sorry tale. Retri-
bution properly begins as the Princess offers her a position in her
household. The attendants gather around to restore her beauty
and to dress her in fine clothes. She tells Tsai-Yong that if he
wants she will remain as his consort during his new marriage.
However, such a sacrifice is not needed. Tsai-Yong chooses to
return to his wife, and the Prince will ask the Emperor to
rescind the royal marriage.

It would seem that Howard's and Irwin's adaptation of the
ancient legend is fairly accurate and reliable. Certainly, there are
a number of situations present which have the familiarity of other
universal stories of a similar pattern. However, aside from the
technical innovations which Howard welcomed, there is actually
little in the material itself to attract a modern, occidental audience. Given, as it were, plain, it has obvious, limited appeal. These
are probably the reasons for the lack of a New York production
until sixteen years later in 1946, when an exceedingly expensive
production could be mounted, making it into something essentially different—a kind of spectacle-pageant. Here with the

best talent Broadway could offer—Mary Martin, director John Houseman, designer Robert Edmond Jones, music by Raymond Scott—the simple play is barely visible at all, a fact which probably accounted for the successful long run.

The critics talked about this neglect, pointing out that the dramatic material was "not clearly woven." The story was simply overpowered by the pageantry, which was uniformly agreed to be exceptional.[3] John Chapman was quite direct in his placing of the story: "Life is not in the telling of its story, however. The telling is a selfconscious attitude which doubtless is arty as all hell but which reminded this oaf of the annual June play at a girls' school."[4] Louis Kronenberger cited the great difficulties with such material, granting that the spectacle approach might be the answer. Possibly, he suggested, a pictorial ballet might even be better. The writing "approximates (though it never quite achieves) both the sought-after simple style and the sought-after formal style. In brief, it serves." And because the story is submerged and broken up, it never becomes "dramatic or affecting enough."[5] There is an irony in the fact that Howard closes out his career (the last Broadway opening) with a successful pageant, considering that the career began with pageants and masques in 1915 and 1916.

II   The Late Christopher Bean (*1932*)

By 1932 Howard had turned out a wide variety of translations and adaptations of foreign plays, none of them successful, and nearly all, he admits, done strictly for commercial reasons. *The Late Christopher Bean,* however, became the one notable successful adaptation from European literature.[6] The difference here may well have been the obvious attraction of the original material. René Fauchois' play, based roughly on the life of Vincent Van Gogh, was a major success in Paris; Emlyn Williams had already written a version for the London stage; and now Gilbert Miller urged Howard to do the same for the American stage. With Howard's long interest in music and painting this was obviously a joyful commitment. A year earlier he had begun *Alien Corn* (1933), a study of a musician's life; now with the new task he could immerse himself in the arts in general.

The comedy takes place in rural, Yankee America outside of

Boston. The household consists of the "undistinguished" rural M.D., Dr. Haggett, his wife, and two daughters. They are served by Abby, a Yankee villager of "indeterminate age." The opening scene is an excellent, simple arrangement for good domestic comedy: it is early morning, the doctor arrives from an early hour case, breakfast is readied by Abby, the others come in; and in short order all the bustle and bother of their lives comes tumbling out. Today Abby is leaving them after fifteen years; all are distressed except Mrs. Haggett who would rather have a more proper maid anyway. It seems Abby, in the characteristic Yankee manner, is less a servant and more a member of the family. Or at least, through the years, she has—despite Mrs. Haggett—made herself one. As she tries to hold back her tears, Abby keeps saying that "it's the will of God," that she must help her brother with his four children now that their mother has died. Abby is quickly established as an essentially simple but earnest and determined woman.

Conversation turns to additional distressing news as the doctor announces that times are bad and they can't afford a Florida trip this year. Mrs. Haggett is adamant, contends that the daughters, Susan and Ada need the exposure for their social chances. The following good exchange is in the vein of the Bennet family in *Pride and Prejudice*—the same universal search for husbands for unmarried daughters:

MRS. HAGGETT: Them Miami beaches is just alive with boys who don't give a thought to nothing but romance and getting married.
DR. HAGGETT: Most boys get them ideas most any place.
MRS. HAGGETT: Not in New England in the winter time.

The doctor's insistence that the village boys are all right fails to convince Mrs. Haggett and particularly Ada, the older daughter. Abby volunteers that she's crying about leaving and they are doing the same about staying. Siding with Dr. Haggett simply raises more friction between Abby and Mrs. Haggett, but then she has always said her piece in family squabbles.

The central plot concerning the late artist—and sometime Haggett boarder—Christopher Bean is established in a careful sequence of events. First, a telegram arrives for the doctor.

saying that an admirer of Bean named Davenport will call during the day. We learn that at one time the struggling artist lived with them, but not much beyond that is said. The entire matter of art and painters is rather deftly moved into the center of the action without any lessening of interest in the domestic involvements. The young village painter, Warren, serves as the catalyst. Both an artist and a house painter, he is currently doing some redecorating in the house. He is also the silent suitor for Susan. In his offer of small paintings (a fish and a duck) to the daughters and in the mother's swift refusal to hang them anywhere, we are brought directly to the subject of art.

Mrs. Haggett, alert to all possibilities in the husband chase, sees Warren as a possible prospect—but as a house painter not an artist. She would rather he paint the fence than the girls, which he had offered to do. In some quick, trial sketches, which are admired by Dr. Haggett, we learn that Christopher Bean helped him in his painting when he was a boy. Everyone is also surprised that Abby reveals a familiarity with artists' tricks and habits. (All of these, of course, are clues to the final denouement.) When Warren's interest in Susan is revealed, Mrs. Haggett has another fit. With some support from Dr. Haggett, Warren storms out, calling the mother a "Philistine," an anti-artist.

A. *The Artist Restored*

The Bean mystery deepens as a Mr. Tallant comes to the door, is promptly mistaken for the expected Davenport, and proceeds to repay a $100 debt of Bean's owed to Dr. Haggett. At this point, with Tallant's questions about Bean's paintings, we begin somewhat to put the links of the plot together. There are good comic effects here as the family recover old Bean paintings (apparently worthless) used to stop leaks in the chicken house. When Dr. Haggett suggests scrubbing them clean, Tallant nearly collapses. One painting has Ada's painting on the reverse side; Tallant pretends great admiration and offers $50 for Ada's work: "You did this little masterpiece on a few lessons?" Ada gasps, "But I could do one like it every day." Dr. Haggett begins to have suspicions. Abby remains indifferent until a little later when she talks to Tallant alone. Tallant seems to know that she had befriended Bean when he lived there. Her basic simplicity and honesty became apparent in the guileless way she talks of Bean's influence on her life, not realizing that Tallant is probing her about Bean's paintings. She says that Bean taught her how to see the world, "like the rust color the marshes get this time of the year when the sky gets the color of that old blue platter."

Another seeker after Christopher Bean, the art dealer Rosen, comes to the house; he offers the staggered Haggetts $1000 for his paintings. Finally, Davenport, the reputable art critic, arrives and everything comes out into the open. Bean has been declared one of the great masters of all time and the paintings—whatever remains—are worth a fortune. As the visitors finally leave (for awhile) the Haggetts sit stunned trying the figure out what's what. What comes immediately to the forefront is the undisguised greed of both the Haggetts. Although expected in the ambitious mother, it is a little startling in the hard working doctor. Perhaps, Howard is trying to indicate to what extent the Depression years affect everyone. Dr. Haggett even becomes the hypocrite in accusing the visitors. Talking of Tallant, he says, "It's the greed of it that turns my stomach. The *greed!*" The entire family chase around the property trying to find the missing paintings. They all sink when the mother says she burned them. But there is one portrait of Abby in her room and they are determined to get it away from her. An amusing cat-and-mouse game ends the act as they try, with various devices, to get their way with the unsuspecting Abby.

Act Three opens on a conversation between Susan and Davenport; she wants an opinion on Warren as a serious artist. Davenport admits the good Bean influence. More urgent telephone calls come in with museum offers, etc. Haggett admits it's all beyond a simple country doctor. Do they have a fortune or don't they—and where is it? Nevertheless, he is sly enough to suggest the preposterous idea to Abby that they need her portrait to cover an empty space over the fireplace, and that it would be a lasting memento of the affection they have for her. The trick works on Abby and she brings the picture down, and tells a moving, pathetic tale of how kind Bean was to her. The portrait, he told her, was his masterpiece. As they all seem to chorus their affection for her, Abby becomes thoroughly confused and refuses to part with the painting.

By this time, the "buyers" from New York have converged again; and offers, counteroffers, and frantic tempers are jumbled together. While Abby is out of the room, the bidding soars into the many thousands for her portrait. Susan, the honest daughter, objects and Dr. Haggett, beside himself, sends her out of the room. Greed at last reigns supreme. On Abby's return, Dr. Haggett tries to reason her into it: "People in your circumstances ain't got no right to own things that are worth so much money." Even when he finally tells her the truth and offers her a half of the last bid, she refuses. In an effective little speech she tells how she nursed Bean when he was ill—and now he's so famous. The melodramatic wheel turns again when she calmly admits rescuing *all* seventeen pictures from Mrs. Haggett's fire. While the experts verify the seventeen in her trunk as authentic, the question now becomes, Who is the real owner? And then the final surprise, which neatly wraps up the plot (and the seventeen paintings). Abby married Bean secretly years ago; she is Mrs. Christopher Bean! Haggett gives her the paintings as the riot breaks out, and Davenport respectfully bows to her as the curtain falls.

B. *The Passive Heroine*

There is no doubt that the play has a very easy charm about it. We smilingly watch the frenetic goings on of the Haggett family as the promise of great wealth nearly corrupts them. And it is not too difficult at all for an appreciative audience to apply the moral blanket to themselves; the fruit of greed is clearly unpalatable. Of course, circumstances help point the moral, and by the end of the play with Abby's deflating admission of wedlock, all evildoers seem to have an almost welcome second chance. There is that kind of marvelous lightness to the story. Unlike serious drama, we are bothered but never racked by the events. Essential innocence comes smiling through. Abby, one of the more passive of Howard's heroines, simply stays as she is throughout the play; and when all is done, gains prominence we might say, by how far back the others have receded.

According to Bernard Craven, Howard did not do as much with the original play as generally believed. He stays quite close to the basic story, as Emlyn Williams had also done. Howard's major changes are at the beginning and the end. The revelation of Abby as the artist's widow is not in the original or Williams.[7] Howard succeeded admirably, as most critics agreed, in establishing a believable New England setting for the original French comedy. To some critics who expressed doubts about Howard as a playwright because of the demands of the lucrative screenwriting assignments, this play reestablished his reputation.[8] Richard Dana Skinner considered Howard among the three finest American playwrights, O'Neill and Elmer Rice being the others with O'Neill first. "Howard," he wrote, "has the greatest native dramatic ability of the trio and the greatest versatility...."[9]

There was no doubt that by 1932 Howard had well demonstrated his range of interests. Joseph Wood Krutch in 1940 summed up Howard's accomplishments. "He can expound Freudianism in *The Silver Cord*, approach tragedy in *They Knew What They Wanted*, declaim rather intemperately in *Half Gods*, and achieve a serene comedy in *The Late Christopher Bean*. But none is more characteristic of him than the rest. Neither is there anything common to them all except the rigor of the characterization plus a certain robust delight in the conflict for its own sake. Their unity, therefore, is only the unity of a temperament...."[10] That temperament, of course, is Howard's own—quick, vigorous, ever direct, and bristling with life.

III   Alien Corn *(1933)*

A personal love of music is obvious in *Alien Corn*; the play is filled with the specifics of the profession.[11] It is no accident that this play appears at this time, within a few years of his marriage to Polly, daughter of the world famous musician, Walter Damrosch. An even closer reference exists since Polly herself is a concert pianist, and we thus have a complete parallel with the father and daughter of the play. Although generally thought of as a story of "the artist life," it can also be seen as a story of college life and a story of homesick Europeans.

The setting is a small Midwestern school for young women, Conway College. For two years, Ottokar Brandt and Elsa Brandt, father and daughter, have been in exile from their beloved Vienna. Their history is a sad one but probably believable considering the strong anti-German feeling in World War I: they were

interned in Georgia, the mother died of influenza, and the father's
unsuccessful suicide attempt left him with a paralyzed arm. Now,
in better but frustrating circumstances, Elsa teaches music—and
Brandt grows more restless for the Old World. The opening
scene has other faculty members helping the Brandts as they set
up things in a new college residence. The occasion is convenient
in introducing various issues as family pictures are passed
around. There is even one of Brahms inscribed to Brandt who
had been a violinist in his day. The picture of the mother, who
had been an opera singer, brings the following from Brandt:
"She and I stood among the great ones of the world. Now she is
dead and I am finished and only the child remains. But the child
will stand among the great ones too!" For a first speech (and
part presentation of the theme) these words are a bit pompous,
and nearly unrealistic. On the other hand, they may well represent Howard's attempt to catch the Teutonic idiom. Throughout
the play, Howard relies heavily on numerous German
exclamations.

Elsa yearns for a chance to prove herself in the concert world
the way her parents have. Although only twenty, she carries
herself with an air of authority. The terms of the description
("high carriage," determination) mark Elsa as another strong
Howard heroine. We are not then surprised (and possibly sense
a plot point) in meeting her lover Julian who seems nearly the
opposite in temperament and physical condition. Julian is the
over-worked, under-appreciated English instructor. They had become lovers the previous summer, possibly a momentary idyll
in the country. Elsa cautions him on his present, romantic
enthusiasms.

ELSA: I still believe in my star, Julian. I need all my strength for
my faith in that. I haven't any left over for you. Or any other man.
JULIAN: No one your age has any right to be like you.
ELSA: No one like me has any right to be my age!

This is a marvelous exchange: one of the few examples of Howard's reliance on the cleverness of language alone. Little else is
needed, at the outset, to establish their differing natures. The
additional fact that the pompous senior English professor, Skeats,

is able "to push" fifty exam papers onto Julian's lap to correct, tells us more. If Elsa is to be the heroine of these few events, Julian will be the victim.

These opening views of college faculty life are general enough to be accepted. The various types would fit the public's view of hallowed academia. Professor Hubert Skeats probably fits the mold for many instructors that Howard knew at Berkeley and Harvard who begin to have a prominence outside the college walls. Skeats gives radio readings in drama and is evidently building a wide, appreciative female audience. He has his way with the hapless Julian by promising him his old course, which would advance him. In addition, we get the grimy side of campus politics when Skeats holds Julian's radical lectures over his head. Howard's ironic intentions with Skeats are played up in his professed ecstasy over the new occupants of the house: "When I consider this house," he tells Elsa, "where music and literature are bedfellows. . . ."

A. *The Defensive Artist*

The introduction of Harry Conway, son of the college's founder, into Elsa's confused affections offers a nice complexity to the plot. She is trying so hard, out of her general pique, not to like him; but, of course, she eventually accepts him. It is the old battle, rather well illustrated here, of the artist versus Main Street. What makes their early differences particularly amusing is that she is determined to expect the worst from a businessman. The self-defensive, hypercritical attitudes of both father and daughter, according to Krutch, often mislead our sympathies. The apparent adversaries to art are not entirely unattractive: "So far as humanity was concerned, these Middle Western provincials came out pretty well from a comparison with the fine flower of artistic Europe."[12]

This is not to say that these feeings about the play are what the playwright intended. It is obvious that we are meant to cheer for Elsa as she does battle with the college authorities. The suggestion that she propose herself as the recipient of an unfulfilled music scholarship seems like a marvelous opportunity, which she accepts. The melodramatic ups and downs follow in the granting of the award, which they all toast, and then the withdrawal on grounds that she is not a Conway graduate and not of American birth. Brandt accuses the administration of cruelty: "You are strangling my daughter's talent." However, it must be remembered that the specifics of Elsa's unrest ("the strength failing in her hands") would be far more acceptable if they were somehow dramatized. As it is, all we have are the words. Although it is true that her personal appeal to Conway has a good theatrical effect—even more so as delivered by the capable Katherine Cornell—how much better it might be if we could see for ourselves what is troubling Elsa. "A demon child that's got to be born" makes a fine phrase but it is isolated; there is no context that we can really fit it into. Here again, as in other plays, Howard relies on general truths about the artist's woes. It seems far easier for him to establish the predicament than the characterization.

A solution to the dilemma is offered; they will have musicales in the house and thus raise the money. Elsa will play the piano and Conway's wife, Muriel, with some musical talent, will sing. All the faculty supporters take up the idea and believe it will work; a noisy discussion follows as to what music would be appropriate, and through all the hubbub the note of a business sense is clearly missing. (We have the feeling that Andy Hardy putting on a school show would have a better chance.) What does begin to thrive quite quickly is the romance between Conway and Elsa. The scene that develops this complication is rather well planned. The level of the conversation moves from hesitant doubt through intriguing sparring to final conviction. There is a good modern, sophisticated tone in Elsa's reluctance to admit her passion: "Why did you have to do this to me? Just now? Why couldn't you leave me to work?" Conway says that his marriage to Muriel had failed years ago. Nevertheless, as Elsa admits later to her father, she wouldn't step between them. Somehow, this becomes a sacrifice on her part to her devotion to music.

A subplot involving Julian is developed further. Early in the play he had been disgusted with a teacher's life, and was decidedly restless. On the advice of a colleague he took up pistols. Now he bursts into the scene, waving the pistol and crying that he's "born anew," that becoming a marksman has changed him. Rhapsodically, he courts Elsa again: "Take wing with me, Elsa, and fly through spiral nebulae and be mine...." Matters are somehow moved down to a less exotic plane, and soon earnest plans are being made for the concert. It seems Muriel, suspicious of Conway and Elsa, plans to sing more and have Elsa play less. An excellent scene then develops between these two antagonists. In the fine line between warranted anger and politeness, Elsa truly reveals her independent, superior strength. Realizing the pathetic position of Muriel in her need to impress Conway, she agrees to accept any program. However, even sacrifices are hard to establish: Muriel talks on and on about their loveless marriage while Elsa vainly tries to back out. A good comic interlude closes the act; Muriel in rehearsal becomes harder to take than Muriel in love. Father and daughter hadn't realized how "frightening" her voice is. Partly in German, Brandt bursts out that in his house no one sings Schubert so badly. Muriel attempts "Depuis le jour" and the E natural ruins her. Father explodes again. Muriel runs off, certain now of the attachment of Elsa and her husband. Elsa is determined, as she embraces her father, to get ahead on her own.

The last act opens on the evening of the concert. The faculty is impressed, the music is excellent, but only thirty-nine attend. Julian uses the sad occasion to push his suit. "She's had her chance! Now give me mine! I'm sorry my chance has to be bought at the price of hers, but I'd be less a man, a good deal less, if I didn't rejoice in it at any price!" Elsa remains unmoved by it all; she knows she played well and decides to continue to give concerts despite the personal financial loss. She wants no help from the administration. However, the administration, through Mrs. Conway's intervention, now wants her resignation. Elsa's supporters crowd to her defense, offer to sign a petition on her behalf. The condition, which she gives in to, will prevent her from hiring halls for future concerts. "Now we won't have to fret any more." Elsa tells her father. "Just sink into things."

Julian urges her to leave with him. Defiantly, he throws the corrected papers into the fireplace. He realizes that Elsa cares for Conway. In the final desperate scene Julian waves his pistol around the group, unsure what to do. Should he shoot Conway?

Would that help Elsa? He turns quickly away and kills himself. While the police gather and ask their questions, Elsa surprises Conway by announcing dramatically that she can't marry him, that she's not a teacher any more, that the piano is her life! Her home, she tells the officer, is not here, but in Vienna.

B. *The Critics*

Generally, the reviewers liked the play; certainly, they all admired Katherine Cornell in a virtuoso performance. Miss Cornell had purchased the play for her own production, and had undoubtedly realized what a strong star play it was. This may well account for some of the superlatives from discreet reviewers such as Brooks Atkinson. He said that in every respect it was "a superb bit of theatre." Although drawbacks in the writing are obvious, Atkinson still hailed the production as a "perfect union of playwrighting and performance."[13] Along the same vein, Morton Eustis seemed willing to accept the play as it was without any illusions of greater worth. He granted the old clichés, the type characters. Howard, he maintained, "like Miss Cornell, knows the theatre from the bottom up and when he resorts to tricks they are effective dramatic tricks. *Alien Corn*, in short is 'swell theatre' in the language of Broadway."[14]

Commonweal, rather perceptively, made the case that the struggle of the artist is not the essential theme. "*Alien Corn* is a play about homesick people who happen to be musicians. It is distinctly not, as many criticisms would lead you to believe, a play about musicians who happen to be homesick." What actually results may be the theme of "eternal homesickness inspired by the struggle of dreams against reality." And since, as it appears, there is confusion in the story, Howard may well have "lost the soul of his own play."[15] Howard's difficulty is in the portrayal of the struggling artist, even upon conventional lines. One of the first to point this out to him was his close friend (and critic) Barrett Clark. Howard particularly wanted comments since Clark's wife was a pianist. Their reaction was uniform: "The play didn't ring true" (Clark, p. 207). Not happy with their report, he nevertheless cut much of the early draft.

The popularity of the play was probably due, ironically, to the general audience's limited knowledge of the artist life.

The bare outlines of the usual plot (the artist versus Main Street) would, in all likelihood, suffice. It was in that sense, then, a plot that the audience wanted to believe. A sentimental championing of the artist could be taken for granted. The fact that Elsa rides rather hard on the college community seems incidental as long as she protests enough—which she certainly does.

IV   Dodsworth *(1934)*

It was a happy arrangement all around when Howard and Sinclair Lewis agreed to make a dramatization of Lewis's phenomenally successful novel.[16] The subject matter—the adventure of Midwesterners in Europe—was well suited to Howard's interests and abilities. The opportunity was readily there to bring to life the restless, vain Fran Dodsworth and the earnest, if at times befuddled, Sam Dodsworth. In essence these were the kind of people Howard had portrayed before—essentially simple people caught up in a faster pace than they had ever known before. Moreover, few playwrights were as familiar with the European settings as Howard, the inveterate traveller.

The structural plan for *Dodsworth* is somewhat like *Half Gods* with a large number of brief scenes. The opening scene is in the Midwestern town of Zenith, in the office of the president of the Revelation Motor Company. A cleverly designed set by Jo Mielziner reveals a vast, square-paned window through which we see the roofs of the plant and the skyscrapers of the city. It made an effective opening tableau to have the curtain rise on Sam Dodsworth as he stands at the window, his back to the audience. In arrangement, the effect is nearly identical to the initial view of the aviator in *Bewitched* as he stands before the large garden window of the French chateau. Here, however, our hero is not to "break in" but (in a sense) to "break out" of his surroundings. It is the day of Sam's retirement and he is about to say his farewells as president and begin his long awaited tour of Europe.

Last minute preparations continue at home; Fran is nearly exultant about the trip, consoles Sam that a new life awaits them, that they will have it "all over from the beginning." Despite the mixed feelings of twenty-five years in his business,

Sam begins to feel consoled in Fran's enthusiasm. The tenor
of her strong desire to escape the Midwest is reminiscent of
Lewis' most famous heroine, Carole Kennicott in *Main Street*
(1920), who felt culturally orphaned by small town life. Fran,
who is thirteen years younger than Sam, at thirty-nine, makes
an impassioned plea for her rights: "And I want the lovely
things I've got a right to! In Europe a woman of my age is
just getting to where men take a serious interest in her! And
I just won't be put on the shelf by my daughter when I can still
dance better and longer than she can! I've got brains and, thank
God, I've still got looks! And no one ever takes me for more than
thirty-five—or thirty, even! I'm begging for life, Sam! No, I'm
not! I'm demanding it!"

A few days later, at sea aboard the *Ultima*, life indeed seems
to be overflowing for Fran. At the Captain's dinner on the last
night out Fran is surrounded by gay, bright, sophisticated talk.
The device is somewhat trite yet still convincing. Young bride
says to husband, "I want another gin fizz, darling." Young bridegroom replies, "You've had enough gin fizzes, sweetheart."
Equally concerned with Fran's welfare is the newly-met Major
Clyde Lockert of England. He announces plans that he has for
them in England, although it is obvious that the debonair
Britisher has already set his sights on Fran. Sam's excitement at
seeing land scarcely moves the phlegmatic Clyde. As they go
out to dance, Sam heads for the bar to toast the landfall.

We are not at all surprised, considering the fast pace of the
scenes, that immediately Sam meets someone for himself. Mrs.
Edith Cortright is an American expatriate living in Italy. It
seems surprising at first that the world-travelled Mrs. Cortright could have much to say to the almost boorish Sam.
In their initial conversation we have the feeling that she is
being exceedingly patient, perhaps for a purpose. We learn
that she had been married to a Britisher, but now lives in Italy
because "it's cheap." The scene becomes slyly comic when her
provocative remarks evidently miss their mark.

MRS. CORTRIGHT: [on being abroad] Drifting isn't nearly so
pleasant as it looks.
SAM: If you don't like it why don't you give it up?

MRS. CORTRIGHT: [again darkly] One drifts for lack of reason to do anything else.
SAM: What do you want?
MRS. CORTRIGHT: [amused] What do you suppose any lone woman wants?

Sam has been under wraps for too long and is not yet up to the possibilities of the "outside world." In such a predicament, of course, we have the essence of good household comedy since eighty percent of the males in the audience would probably have reacted the same way.

Three weeks later in their London suite, the Dodsworths are riding high with the best of English society. Under the "sponsorship" of Clyde, the Americans are beginning to flourish. More to the point, Clyde presses his suit with Fran: he tells her that he needs her "to spur" his life. Fran replies, "I've read that in books, but it's nice of you to say it." Following what he believes to be the proper cue, Clyde kisses her. The events that follow are rather routine: Fran becomes frightened, Clyde confused; he thought he was doing the expected. He leaves as Sam comes in, warning her bluntly not to start what she can't handle. Completely upset by now, Fran goes to pieces in Sam's arms and confesses the entire Clyde affair. Probably as a fact of his greater maturity (or basic naïveté), Sam sloughs off the entire matter and comforts the embarrassed Fran.

A. *The Parisian Life*

The next stop, months later, is in Paris. The social circle is an ample one again, even including some of the friends on shipboard—Mrs. Cortright and others. Mme. de Penable urges Fran to take a villa at Montreux for the season. The talk—particularly of the Europeans or the expatriates—is very chic and worldly. Sam, just back from sightseeing, is overwhelmed by what he has seen. To sit, for example, where Napoleon sat is very exciting. Later, in conversation with Fran, he admits a restlessness with these people, the Parisian smart set. Fran hotly defends them: "They are the most amusing and exclusive crowd in Paris." She wants to do what the right people are doing. She even shocks Sam by telling him that she is tired of apologizing for him, that only in Zenith is he a big man. Sam counters with a good defense of the better civilization, the American civilization: "Maybe clean hospitals and concrete highroads and no soldiers along the Canadian border come nearer to my idea of the real thing!" Somehow, a little abruptly, we find ourselves well into a major confrontation between Sam and Fran on the merits of the Old World. Fran is determined to get the most out of her time in Europe; she decides to take the Montreux villa. When Sam expresses not unreasonable fears about their marriage and agrees reluctantly to stay on, she urges him to leave. In a major speech—what with Howard could be called the "speech for freedom" that we have heard elsewhere—Fran declares for complete independence, or at least, enough time to be alone. She wants to find herself; she's not ready for *his* old age. She needs her fling now. Sam makes plans to leave.

Briefly, we are back in Zenith again while Sam reappraises what he left behind. Now with his friends, he talks with the old familiarity about business things. Sam has sincere doubts about his new leisure. The scene shifts again to Europe, to the villa at Montreux, where Fran is surrounded by the smart set. While the men press their attentions on her, Fran tries not to be bothered by a letter from Sam which has just arrived. She is urged by Arnold Israel, the current suitor, to live for the moment. He offers symbolically to burn the letter. She lets it happen. Eventually, Sam returns to Europe and the couple meet again in Paris for another decision-making scene. In a very strange, blunt manner, Sam forces a choice between Israel or himself. While Israel stands icily by, Fran tells Sam to his face that Israel has made her feel like a bride, "as you never did!" Again, in a rather unsupported way the scene ends with a reconciliation of the couple. We are supposed to believe that Sam's trump card—the announcement of daughter Emily's pregnancy back home—is enough to pull Fran out of her licentious new life. Even less motivation is given for Sam's wanting the new Fran back.

Months later in Berlin, as the continental whirl continues, we find a grateful but not essentially changed Fran. Baron Kurt von Obersdorf, a sometime member of their travelling "circus," is the new suitor. Fran explains how Sam won her back: "By not

being a Tartar husband. By understanding. By letting me have
fun with nice little Kurt and not thinking that I'm a hussy. By
helping me to forget Arnold Israel. By forgetting him yourself.
That's how you've won me back, my noble, big Sam!" However, by the time the entire scene is played out, the bond snaps
again. Kurt, more serious than Israel, proposes marriage—if she
were free. Elated at the thought of being young again, Fran
breaks with the bewildered Sam and they agree to a Berlin
divorce.

Perhaps by this time we should begin to wonder about Sam's
staying power. He seems to be the constant victim of Fran's
inevitable whims. Now, for the first time we are about to witness
some real independence on his part. The opportunity is in Naples
where he meets Mrs. Cortright again. As her name seems to
indicate, *her* designs begin to materialize and soon Sam has
moved into her villa. Now back in Berlin, Fran meets with Kurt's
mother, the Baroness von Obersdorf, a determined woman of the
old school, who can not accept Fran. Such a setback astonishes
Fran; she even offers to secure a good position for her son. All
to no avail. "Have you thought," the Baroness says, "how little
happiness there can be for the old wife of a young husband?"

Sam's idyll, meanwhile, continues beautifully at the Villa
Cortright Posilipo. In a well developed scene we see a reju-
venated Sam enthusiastic about life again—and openly in love.
In a bit of melodrama their protestations of love are played
out while the phone incessantly rings—and we know it is
Berlin calling. Sam can't say No to Fran's appeal for help, even
though Mrs. Cortright's accusations of selfishness are certainly
to the point. She reminds him that "you were a young man a
minute ago." The scene is effectively dramatized as she tries
to prevent his leaving. Nevertheless, loyalty wins out and he
leaves for Berlin.

The final scene is in Bremen harbor, aboard the *Ultima* as she is
about to sail. We get a quick replay of the initial ship scene with
the smart set coming and going, clinking their glasses, and
nearly the same smart, empty talk. Fran talks on and on to a
silent Sam about all her adventures, being bored with Berlin,
bored with everything. Sam becomes increasingly nervous as the
chatter goes on—and then finally calls for a porter and orders

his bags off the ship. He announces he is not sailing. When Fran in desperation asks what will become of her, Sam answers, "I don't know! You'll have to stop getting younger some day!"[17]

B. *Dramatizing the Novel*

It was not an easy task to bring the large, episodic novel down to a few hours on the stage. Both writers wrote brief essays on the subject that were published with the play. Howard made the comment that it would have been easier to dramatize a lesser novel, one deficient in character and incident.[18] It was of course a bit of over-praise for the novel. Howard was generally inclined to belittle the task of dramatists compared with novelists. Men who wrote plays, he said, are lazy; the actors do the work the novelist has to do. The method Howard used was the same he had used successfully with the scenario of *Arrowsmith* (1931): "dramatizing by equivalent," finding suitable lines and business to represent large units of the book. The two authors, in the few sessions they had together, had already fairly well decimated the original. "I remember," Howard said, "one Lewis slogan from those two days—he spoke it so often it became a slogan. 'What's the idea of this lousy speech?' he would say, and indignantly, too. 'It came out of the book,' I would answer. 'Take it out of the play,' he would answer me back. 'It's no good in the play.' When we had finished there was scarcely a line of the book left."[19]

Sinclair Lewis admitted that many excellent scenes of Howard had to be thrown out. There was, for example, the Notre Dame scene (six lines now in the play) in which we sense Sam's silent awareness of the Cathedral's beauty while the tourists and guides rush by. "It was a scene," Lewis wrote, "at once amusing and impressive—Sam himself as solid and functional as one of the Cathedral columns, silent amidst this mumbling. It would have played. But it was not necessary—and out it came. Yet probably it was necessary to have written it, and completely, before one could be sure whether it should be retained or not."[20] The entire business of dramatizing a novel, according to Lewis, is an act of creation. The close study of the novel is less important "than the process of imaginative reflection which recasts the original elements for the stage."[21]

Howard commented on the problem of Mrs. Cortright who, in the novel, appears only at the end. He had the task of introducing a character earlier in the play who at first has nothing to do. In all, Howard wrote, "I was determined that the play should be what the novel is: a panorama of two Americans in Europe and a great deal more than the breaking up of an over-matured marriage." The results, however, Howard admitted, were less of the panorama and more of the marriage: "We had a marital journey's end in dramatic form." He was not, then, completely satisfied with the play—and he wrote at the time that he would do no more book adaptations.[22] Others, however, felt differently about Howard's accomplishments. Robert Garland wrote that nothing reminds you of the novel, "You do not need to have heard of Sinclair Lewis to respond to it as a play."[23] Arthur Quinn agreed. He wrote that Howard had made a new creation and that the audience will only remember the play and the actor (Walter Huston) and not the novel.[24] Hiram Motherwell said that Howard's singular ability was in catching "the dramatic unity of the novel." The novel itself, he maintained is dramatic: "the last tenth of the novel is better theatre than are most plays."[25]

Taking everything into consideration, it is probably safe to say that Howard did as well as anyone could with the novel. The essential problem, of course, is the range of locations—all of which are necessary if we are to understand what is pulling Fran and Sam apart. Howard tried to focus on the panorama of Europe but discovered in practice that the panorama and the marriage are inextricably woven together. What ultimately brings out the worst of Fran and the best of Sam are their experiences of Europe. It is a moot question as to how many experiences must be dramatized to convince the audience. Certainly, fewer than the number Howard gives. And, of course, correspondingly more depth in the characterizations would have made the entire play far better. However, such selectivity might have been foolhardy; after all, it is still Lewis' famous novel that people come to see. The same sort of obligations to the source material were to present themselves to Howard when he came to take on the greatest book challenge of them all—the *Gone With the Wind* adaptation.

CHAPTER 6

Last Plays ... Yellow Jack

I Yellow Jack (1934)

THE amount of time (six years) and the sincerity of the
research that Howard put into *Yellow Jack* are impressive.[1]
At the time of the publication of Paul de Kruif's *The Microbe
Hunters* in 1926, Howard suggested a dramatization of the
eleventh chapter which tells the story of Walter Reed and
yellow fever in Cuba. Although Howard later was to list de
Kruif as collaborator, de Kruif disclaimed all credit.[2] The play—
in its conception and execution—is rightfully all Howard's. The
research involved the Academy of Medicine in New York, the
Surgeon General's Office in Washington, many trips to Havana,
conversations with survivors and with Reed's widow—all, we can
be sure, done with the kind of dogged energy which had become
Howard's trademark. The years of journalistic work for Hearst,
the almost fierce gathering of material all over the world prepared him well. And the greatest challenge of all was to find
some new method to make these heroic events come alive on
the stage. The net result was a production that was universally
acclaimed as a major contribution to modern theater. "A kind
of minor miracle," the New York *Herald Tribune* said, "it is
almost as if, through the adroit use of lights, visible characters,
spoken words, pause and spacing, and nothing else, life were
given to an article in the encyclopedia."[3]

The method Howard adopted was similar to *Half Gods* and
Dodsworth—an uninterrupted series of scenes. It was a wise
choice for a play that is essentially a documentary, actually a
kind of modern Elizabethan chronicle play. Most of all, it was
Jo Mielziner's novel setting which made everything work. Upon
a comparatively bare stage ("a modern approximation of the
Elizabethan stage"), two simple levels were arranged, the one

above containing a bay which served as the laboratory, and the stage level where a variety of scenes could be played. The twenty-nine episodes could move swiftly at the two levels, changes being indicated by lighting alone so that the effect would be one of continuous motion, the play flowing "in a constantly shifting rhythm of light." Bring in appropriate sounds for the military life—and, of course, competent actors—and the illusion is complete.

The structure follows an envelope pattern, beginning in 1929, moving briefly back to 1927, and then to 1900 where the basic story of Walter Reed is enacted. The opening scene is in the laboratory (the bay) in London. The military scientists are experimenting with monkey's liver to study the yellow fever virus. Various officials including the scientist in charge, Dr. Stackpoole, are rather well characterized in their functions prior to any movement of the plot. We stress these virtues since the easy opportunities to rely on events alone would have trapped the lesser playwright. To some extent, then, we know the true nature of Stackpoole's heroism before it happens. An accident takes place in the lab and the assistant is infected by the virus. Overriding the wild confusion, the calm Stackpoole draws blood out of his own arm and injects it into the assistant. He has had the fever and believes he may still retain some immunity. The action is a sufficient occasion for Stackpoole to give the history of the fight against yellow fever back to 1900. What is remarkable theatrically is the real excitement that is somehow engendered in what might otherwise be lecture material.

The major events themselves need careful handling. For example, Stackpoole is about to take his dog to a distemper vaccination when the idea comes to him that his experience with the infected assistant is essentially the same as the vaccination (an injection of living virus followed by immune blood serum) and that it might be the answer to yellow fever. Unless such a development is handled cleverly enough a shallow level of theatrics sets in, similar to the familiar boredom in watching "the great composer" get the inspiration for masterpiece after masterpiece. Happily, in this case, Stackpoole's "great realization" has a prepared reality. The next step is to plan a controlled experiment. And as he bends over his notes, the light concentrates gradually on his head alone and we have an easy transition into the next scene.

The accompanying sound of tom-toms brings us to West Africa in 1927, to another laboratory. The purpose of this scene is to dramatize the discovery of the growth of the yellow fever virus in the monkey. Doctors Harkness and Stokes make the discovery. As Stokes makes reference to the earlier 1900 discoveries ("I wonder what Reed would have said"), light and sound devices bring us to the main setting of the basic story— Havana in 1900. (Obviously, these two outer envelopes to the main plot are primarily cinematic devices.) Immediately, we are introduced to the four heroes, O'Hara, Busch, Brinkerhoff, and McClelland. Of course, they haven't volunteered as yet to aid science, but Howard is wise to establish their characters from the very start. O'Hara is the poetic young Irishman from Galway; Busch is the intense "City Jew"; Brinkerhoff, the Ohio Valley farmer; and McClelland, the "commonplace member" from the South. The representations seems conventionally standard for any story of military life. The setting is the American army in Cuba, where the death list is growing daily from yellow fever— which is commonly referred to as "yellow jack."

The principals of the action and the issues are carefully dramatized. In the Medical Military Commission we have conservatives such as Colonel Tory who is almost ready to give up the fight to save the name of science, and also the wild enthusiast Jesse Lazear, strongly reflective of Howard himself. The issue is the conquest or control of yellow fever if the Panama Canal is to be built. General comment is that it was yellow fever and not the Rough Riders that defeated the Spanish two years ago. Lazear argues intently with Tory: "All right, one thing more and I'll shut up. We're not going home! We're not going to say: 'humanity and knowledge can both go hang, because we haven't got the guts to exceed instructions!' The hell with instructions!"

A. *The Human Test*

In a kind of calm desperation, Major Reed suggests that the only way to test the mosquito possibility is on the men. The response is properly a dramatic bombshell. Carrying on stage the dying Major Cartwright intensifies the effect. Lazear favors the mosquito theory which was advanced by the older Dr. Finlay nineteen years ago. Finlay concedes reluctantly that the only true test will have to be on men. Lazear volunteers but fails to become ill. Carroll tries next and they believe he is infected. The doctors are as confused as ever and the clue hunting continues. It should be obvious by now that there are special theatrical problems when the antagonist for the dramatic action is nearly invisible even to the fine eye of the microscope. As *Stage* pointed out, the situation can nevertheless "call forth a strange and glorious kind of dramatic conflict. . . . If there is one thing that differentiates our age from the age of antiquity, it is the faith in experimental science."[4] And such faith demands successive tests; to clarify the effect on Carroll they test Private Dean. Lazear meanwhile becomes fatally ill. Heroic to the end, Lazear writes his notes, frantically unsure what his sacrifice will prove. At his death the soldiers respond as in a Greek chorus:

McCLELLAND: He was still alive at sundown.
O'HARA: When was it he went?
BRINKERHOF: Just now it must have been.
BUSCH: I seen 'em coming back when it was over. Walking and looking at the ground.
O'HARA: A young man and a great one!
BUSCH: I never met him.
BRINKERHOF: I won't never forget him but I wish I had something to remember him by.
McCLELLAND: It's a tough thing to die. It's a tough thing to die like that.
O'HARA: Us medical men have no regrets dying for science.
BRINKERHOF: And for humanity, John.
BUSCH: Humanity. Yeah. That's what us revolutionaries die for.
BRINKERHOF: He died useful just like he lived. It must be a grand thing to be useful.
O'HARA: There's no end to the glory of sacrifice for science!

The order now goes out for volunteers at three hundred dollars per man. The four soldiers weigh their decision. "I'm tempted!" O'Hara says, "Holy God, I'm tempted!" "It's the very sum of money I been praying for!" Busch admits. Finally, in a burst of enthusiasm, all four agree to do it for nothing, "for the hell of it!" When they report to Carroll, his reaction is pure frenzy and standard melodrama. While the blast of "Stars and Stripes Forever" fills the stage, Carroll shouts, "Did you hear that, folks! Did you see it! We're off and nobody can stop us now! We've got heroes to answer 'em with now!" We have, of course, heard this kind of cry in Howard before; it could be called the defiance-to-the-winds speech, with which the various heroic principals climax the action. The last line is usually something to the effect of "Who is going to stop me!"

The experiment is conducted successfully with the four volunteers. The tide of the melodrama rises and falls as they await the results. The brass band in the background punctuates the good news. The doctors talk of the future and those who will develop a vaccine. The final scene presents Harkness on one side who gives some final facts on the West African lab work; and on the other side, Stackpoole speaks for London in 1929 where the yellow fever vaccination is finally established.

B. *Total Theater*

Apart from the obvious melodramatic effects, the play well deserved its critical acclaim. Technically, it was the most advanced production Howard had ever tried. The complete reliance on light and sound effects nearly approaches what we today call expressionistic theater. Such an ensemble arrangement whereby any means are justified by the desired total effect indicated an awareness of total theater more often seen in Thornton Wilder or Eugene O'Neill. No other play, Howard wrote to Barrett Clark, "gave him more trouble or took more time." It was a challenge to "be exciting without love interest, and heroic without heroics."[5] Fundamentally, of course, the critics were praising a seasoned veteran of the theatrical wars who knew a number of practical things abut his audience. As John Mason Brown pointed out, Howard is "not above running up the American flag when he thinks he needs it, playing taps to guarantee a flood of tears, and closing many of his scenes with good old tag lines."[6]

As a human document, the play has stood up well during the years. It has long been a favorite of the college and community theaters. A 1947 Broadway revival did surprisingly well. Katherine Cornell, in a list of her ten favorite plays in 1957, included *Yellow Jack*. The popular interest, quite rightly, belongs with the subject matter, considering the obvious fact that records of human victories against illness are rarely exciting. Even a lesser play in 1934 on this subject would have had some hearing. That Howard's play is genuine literature has never been questioned. Joseph Wood Krutch explains: "It is unmistakeably literature because it includes implications and overtones and echoes which no simple expository phrase could possibly manage to include within itself, and which would evaporate if any attempt were made to explain them one by one in an essay."[7]

II   Paths of Glory *(1935)*

It is not at all unusual that the ambulance driver and aviator of World War I should want to write a war story. It is even a bit surprising that he waited eleven years after his initial success in the theater to make the attempt. *What Price Glory* (1924) and *Journey's End* (1929) were, of course, the great models to keep in mind. The actual, historic events upon which the story is based were known to Howard before Humphrey Cobb's novel appeared in 1935. The sensational account of the execution of French soldiers for mutiny during the war and the recent reversal of the court martial had been in the papers. They were the sort of terrifying documents of human nature that the idealist Howard could easily fasten on to. *Paths of Glory,* then, can be thought of as a very personal statement despite the fact of adaptation.[8] What then, we may ask, made the New York production such a dismal failure?

According to Arthur Quinn, it was not really a play at all, but "a series of scenes cluttered with characters who rarely become individuals." There was too much of the novel and not enough of Howard. It needed a tragic viewpoint and not the realistic.[9] Following the novel closely committed Howard to the realistic. In the Foreword, Howard admitted that the play is not a creative piece of work. "What was wanted . . . was a setting forth of Mr. Cobb's own scenes as he wrote them, without comment or embellishment."[10] It was hoped that the power of the terrible events would speak for themselves and make their

own convincing case against the senseless acts of the military
machine. As Howard himself pointed out, the audience instead
became angry at the playwright. Perhaps, he continued, it was
not the best time for anti-war opinions. "The cause of peace is
of all causes the one most befailed by lip service." Everyone
is against war but—. We still think of war as a "hero factory."[11]

The play is presented in seventeen scenes, depicting forty-
eight hours in the spring of 1915 in the army zone in France.
The battle weary unit, the 181st Infantry Battalion has just been
relieved of a long tour of duty. We meet representative soldiers
and hear enough civilian talk to have the proper feeling of dismay
and frustration in the hardfought, standstill war. In contrast to
the novel, the three eventually accused and executed soldiers
are introduced early. Langlois is a recently married, intelligent
young engineer who joins the regiment as a replacement. Didier
is a much decorated veteran, father of four. Ferol is a Parisian
Apache with a long list of crimes and vices. Didier has his own
personal nemesis, Lieutenant Roget, from the same village. Later
on patrol, Didier has good reason to accuse the officer of
cowardice and murder; which, however, is not believed. We
have good opportunities, then, to know the three men well—and,
as good drama demands, to believe in them. For example, there
has been sufficient characterization of Langlois so that we can
accept his idyllic "prescription" for staying alive: "If you can't
believe love protects you, though, life isn't worth living."

The division commander, the battle hardened General Assolant,
is told that they must take Hill 57 at all costs. According to his
superior, General de Guerville, the clearing of this obstacle could
be the start of a general offensive to end the war. Assolant
finally consents on the promise of a corps command. The nature
of their "consents" is a clear key to the obstinacy that will
bring on tragedy: Assolant says, "I've never failed to take any
position I promised to take"; and de Guerville replies, "I've
never made any promise I didn't keep." The decision to use the
tired 181st, commanded by Colonel Dax, is the first step in the
perilous chain of events. As we move closer to the time of the
assault the scenes alternate between the soldiers and the command officers. On the one hand we have more of the realities of
soldiers' life, and on the other, more of the intrigue and politics

of high command. At last, the assault is mounted, and as expected, fails. Assolant, furious, is insistent that the men did not move out promptly; he orders the arrest of the entire regiment.

A. *The Failed Assault*

At first, Assolant demands that one section from each company be executed. Even when this is reduced to forty men, Col. Dax is appalled: "You can't sentence forty men to be killed as you would forty head of cattle!" De Guerville, thinking of possible political repercussions, reduces the number to four. His views on discipline hold a terrifying logic. "In the normal and proper course of things troops must be held responsible for defeat. Precisely as they're decorated for victory.... As to these four men, the whole well being of the army demands their death ... a man shot as an example may be as much a part of the ultimate victory as any of us. His death is his contribution to winning the war." The company commanders are requested to select the four men. Capt. Renouart outwardly refuses and the bluff works. Colonel Dax spurred on by this bravery cries out exultantly, "well, there's one man saved! Now, if you and I can't save the other three, by God. . . ." The high words add up to another Howard defiance-to-the-winds speech. (Compare this, for example, to Carroll's speech in *Yellow Jack* when the men volunteer.)

The court–martial, however, makes all further braveries impossible. Good stage theatrics reinforce the narrow, determined stance of the court. It is certainly easy in this scene to hiss the one side and cheer the other. The melodramatics, however, do not seem to reduce the credibility of the events. The military are adamant in their position and are not above the most obvious bending of legal procedures. Ultimately, the case is lost and the three men, Didier, Langlois, and Ferol are found guilty and shot.

Edith Issacs saw the play as absorbing, "with its own clear truth of situation and action and character."[12] She may well have been completely taken up with the theme (as many others were), which would account for the clear indulgence to obvious production faults. George Jean Nathan, more perceptive in terms of theater, said the play was "too affective," actually angered the audience since there was no release for the anger in the play. Technically, he pointed out, the seventeen scene transitions were more abstract and difficult to take than the similar transitions in *Yellow Jack,* where the brilliant design of Jo Mielziner had accomplished innovative miracles. The audience here was forced to sit in darkness and wait for many of the changes.[13]

Most helpful in all the critical comment is an essay by Clifton Fadiman in which he wisely assesses the matter of adapting novels. Here, he maintains, is the basic flaw in Howard's product —the untranslatable excellence of the novel. Howard, according to Fadiman, misses or overlooks the best themes in the novel, qualities which perhaps are too subtle to be dramatized. What Howard does do is a good journeyman play for the masses; and, of course, the ultimate irony is that the play serves neither the one nor the other, for different reasons. For example, take the character of Assolant. Fadiman writes, "In the play (in order to make everything simple) his motivation is vanity, ambition, the desire to pin some fool button or other on his coat.... In the novel he's far more terrible. Put him behind a desk in Paris— and he becomes Clemencau. He is the military mind; that is to say, the other face, the executive face, of the imperialist-mind, the statesman-mind. He *is* war. He *enjoys* killing. He would have just as good a time on the German side as on the French: his patriotism is a geographical accident."[14]

Howard suggested in the Foreword that the play would be well suited to college theater, in particular where they do mili tary training. He recommended doing the play around a war memorial, such as the noble artillery monument in London at Hyde Park Corner.[15] Professor Lee Mitchell at Northwestern University followed his advice, and a month after the play closed its brief run on Broadway, presented it on Armistice Day at the school. During the week's run, the play became the theater's greatest financial success. Mitchell designed a memorial as the set: "The setting grew up in the form of a semi-hexagon of great steps surrounding a massive hexagonal shaft on the face of which was inscribed the words, "To the War Dead."[16]

III The Ghost of Yankee Doodle *(1937)*

Perhaps, it is suitable that the last play produced in Howard's lifetime, *The Ghost of Yankee Doodle,* should be brimful of

political views and ideas.[17] The play is an amazing contrast to
(and culmination of) a career which almost deliberately
eschewed large ideas. With the exception of *Paths of Glory*,
Howard has concentrated his talent with fair success on dramas
of everyday reality, the practical dilemmas of the human condition. Even in *Paths of Glory* the strength of the play is the
depiction of the military life; the thesis fairly well speaks for
itself. However, here for the first time the principals engage the
issues continually. The play, then, is about their conflicting
views on war, neutralism, conservatism, and liberalism. The
result unhappily, as many critics pointed out, is an overabundance
of ideas, an abstract argument. We have the feeling that what
had been obviously in Howard's mind throughout his career
finally erupts on its own as possible dramatic material. The
nature of the play may also be an indication of some "senior
standing" in American theater and an almost devil-may-care
assumption that he has won the right to try whatever he wants.

The play had been planned as early as 1933; Howard wanted
to show that it is no longer possible "to live the good life as a
liberal American with either consistency or honesty." At first
he was going to use the Iowa farmers' strikes, and made trips to
Iowa and even had a scenario and a first act done when political
changes made it all "old stuff." He began over again, although
he was by now determined that the kind of play he had in mind
would require an actress of great prominence. Although the
actress he wanted, Ethel Barrymore, had announced her retirement in 1935, he waited until she became available. The play,
however, was finished in the fall of 1936.[18]

With an amazing sense of prophecy, Howard set the time of
the play as eighteen months after the start of the next world
war. (This then would have put the play in March, 1941.) The
United States is controversially neutral. The place is one of the
"older Western American cities." The Garrison family is gathered
on Christmas Day. The matriarch is the widowed Sara Garrison,
another in the Howard catalog of distinguished, forceful women.
Her brother-in-law, John Garrison, is Chairman of the Board of
the Garrison Tool & Die Company. Rudi Garrison, John's brother,
is the publisher and editor of the local paper. The play attempts
to illustrate the effects of national policies of intervention or

neutrality on the Garrison family and business. The essential difficulty, of course (which is not really overcome), is to make us thoroughly believe in these people *before* they become completely enmeshed in the issues. A device of the holiday event is to have good friend Edward Callory, one-time U. S. Senator and Old Guard Republican, give a lengthy sermon to commemorate the day. He conveniently labels the principals politically for us, rebukes some, favors the others. Rudi is a "coupon-cutting" Socialist; John's "Unions for Peace" is judged unmanly; Roger (Sara's son) is a faulty liberal. However, he does commend the general family spirit as being so much better than in war troubled Europe.

The plot quickly centers on the startling news that the French have sunk the U. S. freighter *Farragut* "bound for Athens with a cargo of spark plugs." The various political positions are hotly debated. John and Roger compare the effect of war on Harvard students now and in World War I. John's wife, Doris, sides with Callory and against her husband: she's a patriot, wants immediate U. S. intervention. The Garrison plant then comes under attack; it has supported peace movements and civil liberties—all not to Doris or Callory's liking. Rudi reminds them of the irony that his liberal paper can't pay its way and must be supported by the family's conservative business, the tool company. A further issue is introduced with the arrival of Martin Holme and his announcement that the university fired him for lecturing on Marx. Martin is engaged to Joan, Sara's daughter. Martin is convinced that Clevenger's Los Angeles *Eagle* is behind it, Clevenger being a publisher of national importance— and, of course a close friend of Sara.

By this time we have had a rather wide-ranging lineup of political views and family entanglements. Frankly, any more would have made the business of the play unwieldy. As it is, it becomes difficult at times to avoid the sense of arbitrary contrivances. Callory sees the family as a microcosm of world events: "The family's a mirror. One of those old fashioned, bulls-eye, convex mirrors that reflects a whole room reduced and concentrated. You can see all civilization in the family. You can see what's wrong with the world." The immediate major irony is introduced as John announces that the family business may well go under because of neutrality. The military accounts are going down and they have a large note coming due. In three weeks, "we'll be in receivers' hands." But John has a solution: the Italian Government will pick up the canceled orders. Rudi objects, accusing John of "chasing war profits!" John counters by reminding them of the facts of business life: "We liberals have to live in two opposite worlds. Our beliefs in one, our experience in the other." The scene ends with the surprising appearance of publisher Clevenger, who evidently is Sara's secret suitor. He once gave her an ermine coat, she grandly admits, for her virtue—and she kept both.

A. *Power of the Press*

Accustomed to exercising power, Clevenger "establishes" himself in the house with his staff—a secretary and his personal pilot, Steve, an illegitimate son with his own prominence as a daredevil flyer. Clevenger, modelled on William Randolph Hearst, is characterized as a man who confers with presidents; who, in fact, is currently enroute to see Roosevelt about the *Farragut* affair. The abruptness with which international affairs are dumped, as it were, into the Garrison living room is an obvious weakness of the play. More effective is the good light banter between Sara and Clevenger, two old friends with interesting mixtures of affection and regrets. Our attention, however, is moved back to world affairs; the townspeople are rioting and threaten the Garrison house. And Sara, wisely, begins to guess that Clevenger's task with the president is now to move the nation into war through the press. She continues to speak for peace and a moral leadership for the country rather than a military one.

As the scenes develop, we have various issues "debated" by the principals, including a confrontation between Martin and Clevenger on Communism in the universities, a plea by Steve for Roger to volunteer as a flyer, the unrest of the workers in the tool company for a lack of orders, and the issue of Clevenger's suit for Sara. Of course, the suit becomes completely enmeshed with Clevenger's part in world events. Somehow, we are meant to believe that great decisions are being made before our eyes— that even the balance of world survival may depend on the state of affairs between two old lovers. Clevenger asks Sara (the epitome of Howard's strong heroines) to give him guidance, "an omen." Curiously, the "omen" seems to include the fact of the imminent bankruptcy of the family business because of neutrality. And on this—and we hope other larger convictions— Clevenger reaffirms his decision to end the neutrality.

A week later, the issues are resolved. Clevenger's paper has begun to propagandize for war, a matter of "national honor." The labor unrest at the factory is over since war orders seem imminent. Hopelessly, Rudi intends to fight Clevenger with his own small paper. Most surprising of all is Sara's inability to recognize Clevenger's complete intentions. Somehow, she still sees him as sincere and announces she will marry him. Perhaps it is a matter of sentiment over sense. Further events serve to change her mind a few times more before the final curtain. Steve is killed in an air crash. The contrite Clevenger will acknowledge him now as his son, "the first hero of the new war!" Sara finally decides to "go it alone" in her idealism and says farewell to Clevenger.

A play of this kind is certainly valuable in appraising Howard as a dramatist and as a person. The great and noble intentions are obvious, although it becomes another question entirely whether Howard is up to them. The overabundance of material and events—all on a serious and major level—reminds one of Maxim Gorky's *Enemies* (1916), in which the family business is in peril, the workers about to strike, and conflicting ideologies are openly debated. What makes Gorky's play a powerful success is the depth of the characterizations, a feeling for real life similar to Chekov. To accomplish this in a play so openly propaganda is the mark of the supreme dramatist. For these reasons it seems strange that a playwright such as Howard, who has been described by many as always direct and down-to-earth— and never an intellectual—should take on such a demanding task. The play is also similar to Arthur Miller's *All My Sons* (1949). Again, military supplies are involved and the matter of business and basic ethics are involved. The difference between the two plays is that Miller gives his characters moral choices which they must live with and resolve; whereas Howard merely provides a discussion of moral choices.

The critics were quick to complain. George Jean Nathan suggested Howard return to the films where he left his soul; he titled his review, "A-Riding on a Phony."[19] Edith Issacs wrote that the play was not "much more than an illuminated argument about how property, even in the most humane hands, is an instrument of evil and acts as a boomerang whenever the flares of war are lighted anywhere in the world."[20] Grenville Vernon echoed a general comment that there was simply too much in the play, that a novel would have been more suitable.[21]

IV   Madame, Will You Walk? *(1939)*

The most innovative of all Howard's plays was finally completed at Tyringham on August 1, 1939. Cut short by the tragic accident on the farm on August 23, Howard's life in the theater may well have been turning to new and fascinating directions. At first titled "Summer Night," *Madam, Will You Walk?* is a modern retelling of the Faust legend with delightful charm and engaging wit.[22] Considering the long list of realistic plays, such a fantasy must have astounded friends and critics. The possibility of new directions in playwriting is suggested by a comparison with the confusing *Ghost of Yankee Doodle* of two years earlier. Whereas the earlier play failed in Howard's ambitious attempts to "speak out" on political ideologies, the present play succeeds admirably in "voicing" some of his closest held philosophic views. Perhaps, a lighter vehicle is the answer for weighty matters—a truth that had been demonstrated by such provocative masters as Shaw and Behrman.

"He put so much of himself into that play [*Madam*]," wrote Barrett Clark, "that it reads somewhat like an autobiography. I heard in it echoes of his often repeated notions on what is right for a man to do and what is wrong, and the thesis was always something like this: Whatever a healthy and normal human being feels to be right, *is* right. The traditional taboos are usually wrong, and twist men's minds, and create situations that delight writers but bedevil the lives out of most of us."[23] These are familiar views on the pragmatic life which have been demonstrated in countless Howard plays. All the spunky heroines —Amy, Abbie, Christina, Elsa, and Sara—have fought the good pragmatic fight and won. However, here in this fantasy was a

new challenging way to say some old Howard truths—and
perhaps, a better way.

The play takes place at the Coyle residence, a sumptuous
brownstone mansion on Fifth Avenue, New York City. In the
conversation between the cook and the police officer (called
to check on a prowler) we learn about the late Timothy Coyle,
a very wealthy contractor. The light tone is immediately set by
the strange combination of remarks. The officer talks of Coyle's
generosity to the children of the ward. "A gentler, sweeter,
nobler soul," the cook continues, "never went to God from the
confining restrictions of Sing Sing Prison." Before we have
much time to add that up, the supernatural forces begin to
operate. The double library doors open and shut by themselves,
and the big chair in the room moves around by itself and faces
the window. As the curtains "magically" open, the spectators,
dumbfounded, conclude it is the ghost of Timothy Coyle. Coyle's
sister, Mrs. Fanaghy, and Father Christy enter; there is a
mixed reaction to the news of the ghost. Father Christy: "Such
talk is hardly suitable to a good Catholic." Mrs. Fanaghy, who
could be called a ready believer of sorts, whispers unnoticed
to the chair, "Tim, my darling Tim, are you there and have you
a message?" When alone in the room, she goes further, addressing
the chair and cautioning the spirit that if it be her "darling
brother Tim," not to do anything flashy to Mary Coyle. She will
have troubles enough.

We learn that the house has been closed a long while and is
now reopened for the arrival of the daughter, Mary Coyle, who
spends her winters at Castle Coyle, Ballymore, Ireland. Others
arrive, including Judge Moskowitz, to greet Mary who is the
usual Howard heroine, a bit eccentric in her individuality, but
entirely her father's daughter. She has enough strong character
to get what she wants. The Judge warns her not to be a recluse
again because of her embarrassment for her father's imprisonment. "Your father," he counsels her with curious professional
pride, "was the last of the political giants. He was a politician
worth any grand jury's attention." Things are changing: Coyle's
statue has been restored near the bridge he built—all in keeping
with the memorial concerts Mary has been running in Central
Park.

A charming scene follows between Mary and her suitor, the ambitious musician, Dockwiler. His plodding literalness (almost basic stupidity) and her lively imagination make marvelous foils. For example, she relates that when she is alone in Ireland she makes up conversations between the two of them. Dockwiler asks what "they" talk about. With good sensitivity, which probably misses its mark, she replies, "Oh, a new poem I'd just read. Or an old one I'd suddenly find beautiful in a new way. Or things that happen in the world outside and make me angry because one can't think what to do about them. And when I find I'm choosing too many subjects that might not interest you, well, then, we just have a long talk about you." The effect on Dockwiler is more characteristic confusion. As the conductor of the memorial concerts he has his petty complaints, and this is what concerns him most. After the artistic temperament subsides, they are friends again.

A.   The Elusive Dr. Brightlee

At this point, the supernatural reappears. We are surprised at first to find that the spirit in the house is *not* the late Timothy Coyle. What appears just as mysteriously to Mary and Dockwiler is a Dr. Brightlee. "My dear, dear Mary Coyle," he announces with the appropriate flair. "I've been waiting for this moment all your life." Somehow, Mary seems to accept the spiritual presence; Dockwiler cross–examines him for his credentials and then leaves in confusion. Brightlee, now openly the devil, says he's here to help Mary overcome the family disgrace, and find herself. Following the Faustian theme, he offers her "the pact": her soul for his help.

MARY: My immortal soul!
BRIGHTLEE: Don't give it a thought!
MARY: It's quite an item with the Irish!

Quite simply, Mary agrees. Her aim, she tells Brightlee, is to make people happier and New York City better. The theological insurmountables are rather easily cleared in Mary's frankness: "It's easier than I should have thought to get on with you. I'm not at all clear about the life hereafter. I'm terribly clear about this life. You don't seem as bad as you're painted. (*extends her hand*) I'd rather people didn't know."

From here on the fantasy builds with an easy and delightful conviction. Appropriately, strange things happen quickly to Mary to satisfy the pact. Young cabdriver Scupper comes into her life, with intentions like her own to cheer up New Yorkers. Even Mrs. Fanaghy is affected; with a surprisingly found voice she sings Irish melodies as never before. Of course, Scupper falls in love with Mary, and now Mary is confused. Is Brightlee trying to possess his soul also? Scupper suddenly develops a great tap dancing ability. On the lake in Central Park Scupper and Mary admit their love. However, it is the night of the concert, and in quick events a full-scale frantic, riotous scene develops. Out of nowhere the other principals appear, apparently to confront and accuse Mary and Scupper. The nightmarish quality, partly surrealistic—the statue of Coyle comes to life— would probably be deemed Absurd Theater today. (Of course, mass stage hysterics is an old theatrical trick, long before *Hellzapoppin* of 1938.)

Suitably, the next scene is in the Magistrate's Night Court, where the attempt is made to clarify all events, real and unreal. When Mary asks Judge Moskowitz to defend them, the Magistrate has a snappy answer, "the law doesn't encourage the star witness for the prosecution to act as attorney for the defense." The farce is underway. In defense of himself, Brightlee admits that his aim on earth is to put man back in the center of the universe. In a fast paced, major pronouncement, Brightlee and Mary "chorus" their new and shocking way of seeing things. It adds up to good theater. Brightlee says man should be "a law unto himself," and Mary jumps to agreement. And man's destiny? "To be the unique custodian of the heroic," she replies. Confusion again reigns, and the court (and the scene) ends as Brightlee becomes an infernal red glow while the music (Gounod's *Faust*, of course) rises.

The last act continues the engaging talk between Brightlee and his convert, Mary, as they try to defend their views. The others are not certain who Brightlee is—"Satan, seer, or racketeer." A kind of debate follows. "You called me the Prince of Darkness," Brightlee replies. "I accept that title! It's darkest before the dawn. But our Chairman calls me his Animating Force!" The charges are dropped and their fight is apparently won. Mary asks about the future. Brightlee reassures her that in eleven years Dockwiler will be the second Victor Herbert, and Scupper will be a great dancer in London. Both, he says, will be happily married. To her surprise, Brightlee says he wants her for himself. The mixture of the divine and human appeals to him—and what a chance to improve the stock of mankind. Scupper bounds into the room in costume for the night's performance. Dockwiler plays the waltz from *Faust;* Scupper dances. Mary is unsure which of the three to choose. With good, light, almost inconsequential touches, the fantasy ends as Brightlee leaves and Mary chooses Scupper.

B. *The Production*

The shock of Howard's untimely death was so great that the Playwrights' Company was determined to do all they could with Howard's last play. However, the play needed "one more solid rewrite" as Howard himself had told John Wharton and others.[24] It was agreed that Robert Sherwood would do the work, and Sherwood put everything aside to do this last loving task for a good friend. Actually, the task involved the others (Rice, Anderson, and Behrman) as well, and in their memoirs similar accounts are given of the dilemma which set in. They hadn't reckoned, Rice wrote, on the intractability of the widow, Polly. "Every word that her husband had written was sacred, and she miraculously remembered conversations in which the very passages Sherwood wanted to edit had been pronounced indispensable by Howard."[25] Sherwood, nevertheless, stuck to the job out of loyalty alone, even though they made "little headway against that humorless smile [Mrs. Howard] and finishing-school politeness."[26] There is an interesting footnote to the episode if one is overly inclined to fault the widow. It can be found in the perceptive remarks of Behrman as he recalled the day of the funeral. "At the graveside Polly threw a rose on Sidney's coffin as it was being lowered. I have never forgotten the expression on her face—anger and defiance, as if what she had left could not be taken away from her."[27]

To insure the success of the play, the Company went to the

extent of hiring Margaret Webster, the highly respected English director. George M. Cohan, past sixty and nearly retired, was coaxed to take the part of Dr. Brightlee. It may well be that he was privately flattered since the play was so unlike his usual flag-waving productions. The combination, however, of Webster and Cohan proved an error since neither seemed really to understand what the play was about, aside from the fact that Webster was more accustomed to staging Shakespeare at the Old Vic. On the night of the tryout in Baltimore, Cohan, desperate for his familiar props, pulled an American flag out of his pocket on his last line and danced off the stage. The audience loved it but the play failed. On the advice of friends, Cohan withdrew during the tryouts and the play closed.[28] It was to Cohan's credit that on his deathbed, according to Behrman, he sent the Company a check in recompense for the exorbitant fee he had charged them.[29] It was later announced that Cedric Hardwicke would do the part in June in New York, but the war caused another postponement. The New York production finally took place on December 1, 1953, for forty-two performances. Hume Cronyn got permission to revise the play himself. He took out "a lot of superfluous verbiage and rearranged the scenes as he saw fit." It launched the successful Phoenix Theater.[30]

C. A Female Faust

Howard told an interviewer that the play is "a cockeyed version of the Faust legend."[31] There are, however, a number of interesting alterations. Unlike the basic Faust character of the legend, Mary is not seeking her own special knowledge or power; her goal is simply to help mankind. Neither does Mary as Faust destroy the object of her love, Scupper, who is the equivalent of Marguerite. Most intriguing of all is the elevation of Brightlee (as the devil) to a rank far above the traditional one of incarnate evil. Howard's devil seems to stand for some kind of better, ideal human nature which has too long been suppressed by traditional religion and social systems. Brooks Atkinson wondered how Howard could give "the devil credit for all the joy in the world and for civilization in general?" He credited the play as having a "pagan joyousness" similar to Sean O'Casey.[32] Harold Clurman, viewing the play against the difficult depression days of the 1930's, saw Howard's efforts as "a kind of comedic call to courage."[33]

Reversals of this order in the traditional beliefs about the devil are characteristic of Howard's wholly independent attitude toward life. He seems continually intent on "promoting" more earnest relations to modern life. He confided to Barrett Clark that man might win out over his errors by living life more fully than he thought he could. And in the process he would save his soul. "Man's soul, thought Howard, is nothing to trifle with: it is probably . . . his capacity for living life to the point where it hurts. That, he thought, was one answer to the riddle of life—a tentative answer only—but it seemed wholly valid to him at the time, and that was enough for him."[34] The voice of the pragmatist again in Howard: suitable for the moment so why not follow it. A thoroughly modern American habit of living earnestly in the present. Just as well, then, not to probe too deeply in trying to account for the rationale in Howard's theatrical devices. The Faust material is whatever he chooses to adopt for the moment. The fun, then, counts more than any systematic foundation.

The majority of the critics were inclined to judge the play this way. They saw it as a delightful, playful romp into issues of substance—but primarily an imaginative amusement. One called it "minor Shaw"; others saw touches of William Saroyan and Thornton Wilder.[35] Walter Kerr, despite his basic enjoyment, was bothered by the slow pace at times. "There is a disconcerting aimlessness that almost slows the jest to an idle jog," he wrote. Admitting that it was not the best of Howard, it was, nevertheless, "an interesting reflection of an interesing mind."[36]

CHAPTER 7

The Hollywood Years

B Y 1929, at the age of thirty-eight, Howard was at a familiar crossroad in his life. By no means the Broadway novice— three solid successes under his belt—he was still despondent over his broken marriage and unsure of his career. He was, in a sense, ready to be lured into new, more hopeful directions. Hollywood and Samuel Goldwyn beckoned. The filmland mogul was more than generous; he offered to make Howard a millionaire, seventy-thousand a year on a long contract plus royalties on his original scripts. Partly amused, Howard wrote all this to his sister in Berkeley, ending with "Sister, dear sister, I don't need that much cash, do I?"[1] Nevertheless, the association became a long and productive one. At least nine screenplays were written for Goldwyn duing the next ten years, which saw Hollywood becoming more and more an enticing second home. For the most part Howard made it a practice to do his contracted work in Hollywood as quickly as possible and then to return quite eagerly to New York, still the vital center of his writing interests. "I am torn between the West," Howard confessed to Clark in 1929, "where I belong biologically, if you know what I mean, and the East where I am not bored as I am in the West. I miss orchestras in the West, and people, and being near Europe" (Clark, p. 212). The pull of the West remained insistent, nevertheless, to the native Californian, as he wrote Clark in 1931: "Last week I took four days out to drive to and about Death Valley and found it unimaginably magnificent and remote. There is this point to life in the West; you can take three days off, or four or five, or even one, and use them to go to some part which blows your head off and returns it to you dry-cleaned and improved. You can't do that or get that effect from a weekend of rest in Atlantic City, even with the gin in the suit-case" (Clark, p. 219).

In all, Howard wrote thirteen screenplays for Hollywood, ten of which were produced. His first assignment for Goldwyn was to do the dialogue for *Bull Dog Drummond* (1929), the first of a number of vehicles starring another newcomer, Ronald Colman. The film was voted one of the "Ten Best" by the New York *Times*.[2] Other Colman films involving Howard included *Condemned* (1929) and *Raffles* (1930) for which he wrote the screenplays. Another *Raffles* was done in 1940 with screenplay by Howard and John Van Druten. Various awards were won by the Howard films during these years. The high-water marks, of course, were the two Academy Awards—*Arrowsmith* (1931) and *Gone With the Wind* (1939) for the best screenplays. The New York *Times* "Ten Best" was also given to *Arrowsmith* and *Dodsworth*. In time nearly all the Howard plays were made into films, the major omissions being *Alien Corn, Madam, Will You Walk?, Lute Song,* and *The Ghost of Yankee Doodle. They Knew What They Wanted* was filmed three times—1928 (a silent film), 1930, and 1940, with only the 1930 production involving Howard. He was credited with the dialogue and the continuity. Seven other Howard plays were made into films by other writers.

Three completed screenplays became disappointments. An adaptation of *The Brothers Karamazov,* said to be a better script than *Arrowsmith,* was never produced due to a copyright battle which Goldwyn lost.[3] Another Sinclair Lewis "collaboration," *It Can't Happen Here,"* was abandoned because of differences with the Hays Office in 1936 about the propriety of the political views.[4] In 1935 Howard completed an adaptation of Kipling's *The Light That Failed.* For some reason the scenario was put aside and by the time the film appeared in 1939 there was a new screenplay by Robert Carson. The Howard Collection at Berkeley contains a handsome red leather and gilt bound volume of the Howard scenario with prized notes and comments in the margin by Kipling. Evidently, the producer Arthur Hornblow had brought the volume to Kipling for personal comments in 1935. An enclosed letter from Kipling is highly complimentary of the scenario; "enthusiastic," in fact, but with reminders that the language was not as strong as it could be according to the book. The marginal notes are curious reminders of how basically different the two cultures are. Where Howard has written, "So hail and farewell, Torp," Kipling suggests the simpler, "Here's luck, Torp." Similarly, where Howard has written, "By Jove, the boy can draw!" Kipling neatly substitutes directness for the seeming British flair: he crosses out "Jove" and writes in "God."[5]

I   Gone With the Wind

Of all the Hollywood involvements certainly the most fascinating (and rewarding) was the writing of the *Gone With the Wind* script. Today with the continual reshowing of the film, with its monumental box office record, the line "by Sidney Howard" is still up there with the names of the four principals in even the most reduced advertising copy. To many this is still the only recognition of the American dramatist. In the realm of screen writing alone it is a "credit" which many would gladly settle for. Of course, all who worked on the film felt the full complexity of its guiding genius, David O. Selznick. "Complexity" is not an overstatement since every Selznick film was at all times the personal product of this legendary dynamo of the screen. Being on a Selznick film was a strange, torturous, process which gradually managed to unsettle whatever stability there might have been in the lives of the many contributors. The history, then, of Howard's involvement with Selznick is no less a kind of nightmare of its own.

As early as 1933 the enigmatic Selznick was saying nice things about Howard. On beginning his new position at MGM as vice-president, he wrote to Nicholas Schenck, president, that the studio had too many writers. "I should like to see a reduced writing staff augmented with brains of the type of Ben Hecht, Sidney Howard, and Philip Barry."[6] By 1936, at the outset of the *GWTW* production, he had narrowed his choice to Hecht and Howard to do the screenplay. "They are both rare," he wrote, "in that you don't have to cook up every situation for them and write half their dialogue for them" (Selznick, p. 140). In October, 1936, Howard was signed to do the screenplay. From that moment on, their relationship becomes a curious one. Almost immediately they were at cross-purposes. Selznick's "style" was to have his writers constantly available for consultation (and the expected Selznick "collaboration"). Howard's "style" was to hire himself out to Hollywood for specific short periods of time, to do the writing job and then escape as quickly as he could back to the legitimate stage in New York. Their history during the turbulent two years was to be a continual exchange of requests and denials to stay longer in Hollywood. For example, in October 1938, Selznick wanted Howard to accompany him to Bermuda for a work-vacation and one last look at the long finished script. Despite the closeness to New York, the answer was still, No. From Howard's viewpoint, the work was done and the revisions Selznick had in mind were not his concern. As Rudy Behlmer explains it, Howard was "a precise, orderly man who delivered material on time and was used to little interference" (Selznick, p. 165).

Howard's work actually consists of two documents. "Preliminary Notes for *GWTW*" is a fifty-page treatment, thirteen thousand words, seven sequences, dated December 14, 1936. The screenplay, two hundred and forty-two pages, is dated February 20, 1937.[7] When Howard arrived in Hollywood to do the screenplay he was given a copy of the novel with Selznick's marginal comments. For six weeks, he worked sixteen hours a day. The first result was a very long script requiring five and a half hours. Howard cut liberally, rewrote what he had, and left for New York.[8] What happened to the script during the next two years is a rather typical tale in the life of any screenwriter. The work of one man becomes the common property, so to speak, of all the successive writers brought into the project. And, of course, in this case, it was Selznick himself, now as writer, who "chaired" the writing committee. The task was from the start complicated by Selznick's undue reverence for nearly every one of the thousand pages Margaret Mitchell wrote. Howard had earlier pointed out quite wisely that Mitchell had the fault of doing nearly everything in the rambling novel twice. Selznick, nevertheless, set about checking the script against the novel and "substituting valuable lines" wherever he could for "ordinary lines of the script." "I think the most wonderful thing we could possibly accomplish for *GWTW*," Selznick wrote proudly, "would be the announcement that there will not be a single original word in the script that is not written by Margaret Mitchell" (Selznick, pp. 155, 165).

However, as even Selznick himself readily knew, the work of

the professional screenwriter is still indispensable. During these years a long succession of writers was called in. In all they included Jo Swerling, Oliver H. P. Garrett, Ben Hecht, John Van Druten, Michael Foster, F. Scott Fitzgerald, Winston Miller, John Balderston, Edwin Justin Mayer, and Charles Mac-Arthur. A number of these men, of course, are among the most prominent writers of their time.[9] At the time (January 26, 1939) when the actual shooting began, three scripts were in existence: (1) the Sidney Howard screenplay, (2) variations of the original screenplay with new work mostly by Garrett, (3) a Selznick script.[10] Gavin Lambert describes the state of affairs: "It [the shooting script] was still an unresolved mound, pink, yellow, and blue pages indicating rewrites of the original white, but less than a third of the scenes fully worked out and ready to shoot."[11] To complicate things further the director, George Cukor, was fired in February, 1939, and Victor Fleming hired. Fleming immediately called for a rewrite of the shooting script.

Ben Hecht was hurriedly called in for a week's work at $15,000. Although Hecht had never read the novel he was skillful enough to see what had to be done. He suggested they return to the original Howard script since nothing else was as "precise and telling." During that week Hecht worked eighteen hours a day to come up with the final shooting script. On March 1 the filming resumed using basically what Howard had written two years earlier. Of course, Howard did make occasional journeys to Hollywood during these years to do various small things on the project, although never staying as long as Selznick wanted. The last visit for Selznick was in April on a brief dialogue contract. Vivien Leigh wrote to Laurence Olivier April 2, 1939, that things were going badly. "Appalling dialogue," she wrote. "However, David Selznick promises me that Sidney Howard is coming back on the script."[12] Evidently, Margaret Mitchell's sacrosanct words were not quite enough.

The history of the famous last line of Rhett Butler as he walks out on Scarlett O'Hara is of interest and should be included here. Scarlett asks what will become of her and Rhett answers in the novel, "My dear, I don't give a damn." Howard changed this at first in his screenplay to "I wished I cared. But I don't." Evidently, he later had second thoughts and changed the line to the more forceful, "Frankly, my dear, I don't care," and it was previewed this way. The addition of "Frankly" seemed "a minor yet incalculable improvement that would probably never have occured by design" (Selznick, p. 212). Nevertheless, as a result of the preview Selznick decided that the original "damn" was essential. Censor Joseph Breen refused, and Selznick appealed to Will Hays. Hays finally allowed him to say, "Frankly, my dear, I don't give a damn," the line we all hear now. However, since the use was a punishable offense, Selznick had to pay five thousand dollars to the Producers Association.[13]

The film was given its Atlanta premiere on December 15, 1939, some four months after Howard's untimely death. There was some discussion of the screenplay credit. Garrett thought it should be "Adaptation by Sidney Howard and Screenplay by Garrett"; but there were too many others closely involved including Selznick and Hecht (Selznick, p. 216). It was finally agreed to give sole credit to Howard, partly, I would imagine, since it would be his last. *GWTW* received eight academy awards, the most ever given to a film. Howard received his second award for screenwriting, the other being *Arrowsmith* in 1931.

The general critical approval of *GWTW* is difficult to divide. So much of the entire production, including the screenplay, has the energetic, creative mark of Selznick. Whatever was said about Howard's scenario was complimentary. "It is pure narrative," wrote Frank Nugent, "as the novel was"; and properly not a great drama since the novel was not.[14] Remarks of this order were healthy reminders that the workman-like Howard had "translated" Margaret Mitchell's long narrative very sensibly, keeping it essentially at its proper level of good, popular narrative fiction. It was not, after all, Mitchell's intention to write another *War and Peace*. Nugent remarked on the faithfulness of the scenario: it was an "interesting version of the 1037-page novel, matching it almost scene for scene with a literalness that not even Shakespeare or Dickens were accorded in Hollywood."[15]

II *The Art of Film Writing*

From the very beginning of Howard's career as a film writer, approval was generally freely given. There seemed no doubt, from producers and critics alike, that Howard was securely in his element. The high financial return tells us something of his reputation. Individual films were contracted for at the impressive price of twenty-five thousand per, and treatments alone brought fifteen thousand. The few times Howard agreed to be on the weekly payroll at a studio the figure was a very respectable one thousand or fifteen hundred. In 1938 it was as high as five thousand for the week.

In the early talky, *Condemned,* Howard was praised for the restraint with speech: "[he] has economized in words and made the most of silence during the incidents." There was also praise for the construction, the way the film was adroitly "mapped out."[16] The two Sinclair Lewis screenplays were done with the same kind of easy professionalism. On *Arrowsmith*: Howard has done the work "in a knowledgeful fashion with a full appreciation of the limitations of a film."[17] On *Dodsworth*: "Mr. Howard, who must be considered Mr. Lewis' personal dramatic translator, has adapted his play to the screen with the seriousness of an author who has studied his work long and has weighed each comma before fitting it into his literary mosaic."[18]

Characteristically, Howard approached screen writing in 1929 as a challenge and opportunity to raise the level of the new medium. He wrote his sister that the work on *Bull Dog Drummond* allowed him to use his theater experience; it was an opportunity "to teach a motion picture director to lean on a manuscript and take his rhythms and ideas from that instead of picking them out of his own head hit or miss from day to day as motion picture directors have been wont to do."[19] In the pioneer days of the talkies there was much that the new art form had to learn from theater people like Howard. Technical advances from the New York stage, such as revolving stages, were suggested. In a 1929 interview Howard granted the difficulty of writing for a large, wide audience; and pointed to the better scripts being done by the few stage writers "who have acquired a camera-eye technique." The requirements of the two mediums differed: the screen writers "see through only a single lens. We, the playwrights, see through many eyes."[20] Part of the playwrights' larger "eyesight"—by 1932—included adult subjects maturely handled. In an interview Howard ridiculed the twelve-year-old level of contemporary films. Hollywood, he complained, "still operates under the delusion that the screen is for fiction only, that fiction is romance exclusively, that people want only to be anesthetized and that the true, the living, and the disturbing are and must always remain unpalatable."[21]

CHAPTER 8

Evaluations

I *The Modern Woman*

NO other subject looms larger in Howard than the modern woman—brave and defiant, for the most part; but also, at times, incredibly foolish and confused. Continually central in nearly all the thirteen major plays is the one overriding theme of the 1920's and 1930's, the predicament of the newly emancipated woman. The Nineteenth Amendment, Woman's Suffrage, may have become the law of the land in 1920, but the full tidal wave of its effects on literature had been building up since the beginning of the century. In fact, in every generation since the last quarter of the nineteenth century, writers have been restating (for their own times) the fascinating place of women. So, it is not at all unusual that we see essential similarities in the plight of our plucky heroines from the time of Henry James' "Daisy Miller" of the 1870's through Dreisser's *Sister Carrie* in 1900. And, of course, by the time of the American literary renaissance that followed World War I, there was to be a host of gifted writers ready to explain the *newest* of women, the completely enfranchised women, to readers and playgoers.

Howard presents all variations and combinations. What I would call the "brave heroines" are of two orders, the conventional and the liberated. In the same sense, the second broad category, what I term the "foolish" (or the "confused") women, are of two orders, the conventional and the liberated. The question which moves play after play is always the matter of self-assertion, what independent action to take, and to what extent the relative "bravery" can be truly reckoned. And since in theater, as in life, larger events move against lesser ones, Howard provides the full context of such intriguing movements in the characterizations of a variety of women. For example, *Half*

Gods features the contrasting views of two liberated young women, Hope and Helena: with the one (Hope), whose marriage is coming apart, we have the confusion of the basically foolish woman; and with Helena, the divorcée, we have relative wisdom, born, we can assume, out of the hard braveries of experience. Aside from the granted structural weaknesses of this particular play, we do, nevertheless, see the workings of Howard's major concerns about women. In effect, he asks the same questions as James or Scott Fitzgerald: What to do with one's new freedom? What newly placed moral decisions must our new young woman come up with? We find after awhile that heroine after heroine in Howard's plays is somehow able to take some positive (perhaps risky) action—"to confront her destiny" as Isabel Archer magnificently does in James' *Portrait of a Lady*.

Characteristic of Howard, there is a longer list of the "brave and the liberated" than the "foolish and the liberated." Heading such a list might well be the outspoken Christina in *The Silver Cord*, who is able to order her scientific mind into the right declarations of common sense in defiance of Mrs. Phelps' obsessive mother love. Howard chose to add more to the characterization by portraying Christina as a lady scientist, certainly a newer role in the 1920's and one which properly demands conviction and determination. Elsa Brandt, the frustrated piano teacher of *Alien Corn*, also speaks out—this time against the college authorities (representing restrictive life in general); she is determined to make her own way and to be the independent artist. Sara Garrison in *The Ghost of Yankee Doodle* wavers in her major decision but eventually finds the perspective to say "No" to publisher Clevenger's power. Other "brave and liberated" heroines include the fanciful Mary of *Madam, Will You Walk?*; and Bethany Jones, the evangelist who embraces Christ sincerely in *Salvation*, a lesser Howard play of 1928.[1]

All of the above are fairly intelligent, well situated women. They seem to have the necessary requisites (education, professional standing) with which to assert themselves and be the modern woman. There is, however, another type of brave heroine in the Howard canon who is specifically simple and provincial. Amy, the wistful, mail-order bride of *They Knew What*

They Wanted; Abby, the Haggett maid and secret wife of the
artist in *The Late Christopher Bean;* Carrie, the very determined and resourceful tavern keeper in *Ned McCobb's Daughter;*
and Tchao-Ou-Niang, the devoted wife in *Lute Song.* Here,
perhaps, is the essential Howard, speaking out through some of
his most eminent plays in the voices of the plainest of his heroines, possessing, as they do, instinctive gifts of stoicism and
practicality. All of them are the dogged little pragmatists who get
things done, no matter the odds. They are the best examples
in a democracy of the plucky little heroine who will not be
stepped on. Nothing is more characteristically American to a
playwright who always wore his national pride with conviction.
To glorify native instincts at the expense of smooth talkers is
certainly in the popular vein.

The excellent casting of Pauline Lord as Amy served eminently
to bring out such qualities. A common phrase at the time referred
to noted actresses as either "pushers or shrinkers." Miss Lord
was a famous "shrinker," as Joseph Wood Krutch explains:
". . . her peculiar power to suggest the pathos of essential goodness struggling to meet a situation which the intellect has not
been able to think through. It is this essential goodness, coupled
with a native generosity in the girl herself, which make it
possible for the three simple persons involved to face a problem
apparently too difficult for their uncultivated intelligence and yet
to succeed, in a measure, in solving it by means of native virtues
vigorous enough to make them perceive how by giving up
much they can still salvage something from the wreck which
circumstance has brought about."[2] And, therefore, in the most
pragmatic way, led by Amy, Tony the grape grower keeps his
wife, and Joe, the restless man of the road, leaves unscathed—all
getting what they essentially want.

Abby, the dour New England maiden, is another wise party
who keeps to herself. Not by any means as dynamic as Amy or
Carrie, she still manages to shake up the doubtful Haggett
morality when it is most threatened. Again, clear honesty—native
style—wins the day. We are not at all surprised that Pauline
Lord again was the choice for the part. The self-sacrificing
Tchao-Ou-Niang, appropriate to the Chinese classic, is another
rather passive heroine, doing everything humanly possible to

keep the family alive. It is Carrie, however, who seems to have all of God's thunder when the need is greatest. She bustles about the tavern neatly putting people and pretensions in their place; and when the chips are down, the best of her native gifts is there to sort the right from the wrong and keep McCobb's tavern still flourishing. Whatever ethics are involved are, of course, entirely her own, another common characteristic of the type. What counts most is positive action, and we are never in doubt that she will adopt any illegality (in the matter of Prohibition) if her children's welfare is at stake.

On the other side of the ledger are the "foolish and the liberated" women. In company with Hope in *Half Gods* are Carlotta in *Lucky Sam McCarver* and Fran in *Dodsworth*. The list here is noticeably smaller since it is Howard's nature to champion the best of the liberated women and to center his plays wherever inordinate energy and good works abound. However, Howard is sufficiently a man of his times to recognize that the dilemma of the confused modern woman is everywhere. No doubt, many strong feelings about the misspent energies of his first wife, Clare Eames, in her desertion of himself and their child, attached themselves to *Half Gods* and other plays. No one, of course, could really handle the complexity of the type as well as Scott Fitzgerald. We have long marveled at the careful delineation of the rich and beautiful Daisy in *The Great Gatsby* who masks her idleness and boredom with senseless trifles. Fran Dodsworth is cast in the same restless mold. Older, of course, than Daisy, she still suffers from the gnawing doubts of what really to do with her freedom. The opportunities in Europe provide the crucible for a series of bad and ridiculous experiences. She goes from man to man, pathetically unsure what she really wants. Carlotta, on the other hand, is more difficult to appraise since Howard himself admitted that he had failed to make the two central characters—Carlotta and Sam McCarver—human enough. All we can do then is to "read" the bare list of her strange actions as another sorry accounting of misdirected zeal. It is necessary in discussing the modern woman, continually to stress her energy and zest for life, whether for good or ill.

To complete this panoply of Howard's women we should include the few principals who are still very much in the old mode. These people seem entirely unaffected by modern advances in science and psychology. Although not basically evil, they are sorely limited and parochial; they follow a world that does not really exist any more. They confuse the lives they touch. If we consider the following remarks of Sara (*The Ghost of Yankee Doodle*) in her accounting of the "old days," we have some idea of how it is for those who never advance further. "I was put on the stage before I was six and got my picture of life from the plays we played then. They were nice plays and about nice people who lived in big houses in peace and security." Mrs. Phelps, the mother in *The Silver Cord,* is a "nice" person living sensibly, she believes, "in peace and security." Nevertheless, as the play powerfully represents, she is a terror in her children's lives, entirely confused about the bounds of parental love.

Mrs. Haggett (*The Late Christopher Bean*) has an equally limited view of modern life and art. House painters and artists are all the same to her, the only real dividing line being which brings home more money. Muriel Conway (*Alien Corn*) will resort to any means to keep her wandering husband's concern at home. She deliberately ruins the concert that Elsa gives "to emancipate" herself. A defense of one's marital rights is not in itself conventional or foolish; Muriel simply lacks the imagination to do battle with any thing resembling a modern style or spirit.

II *The New Moral Ground*

The critics' choice of the controversial *They Knew What They Wanted* for the Pulitzer Prize of 1925 established an entirely new moral ground for theater. Aside from the usual literary concerns, the clear amoral pattern of the plot was the real and startling winner. Adulterous goings on, whether in one moment of passion or a number, were—in the old style—clearly sinful. Consider then the boldness of a plot in which the "sin" is glossed over as merely a "mistake of the head" (not the heart) and everyone still manages to live happily ever after. How was such a radical change accomplished in the theater? After all, the other sensational play of that year (1924), O'Neill's *Desire*

Under the Elms, despite its overwhelming power and reality, at least punished the sinful Abby for child murder and her "accomplice" Eben, for adultery. Audiences in the 1920's were still ruled to a large extent by the advice of Bronson Howard, prominent American dramatist of the generation before Sidney Howard: "The wife who has once taken the step from purity to impurity can never reinstate herself in the world of art this side of the grave."[3]

Howard's successful method in *They Knew What They Wanted* was a simple reliance on unqualified common sense. Without attempting to lessen the seriousness of the principals' transgressions, he concentrated instead on the realistic aspects of the aftermath, that is, on the extent to which fallible people would make the best of things. There is a baby on its way which two of them want and the other (the actual father) does not want. There is no real love between the erring pair, only the one moment of passion. A characteristic, well respected American way of doing things—the pragmatic way—seems the obvious solution. The pragmatic is not concerned with assigning guilt or debating causes; it deals only with effects. This is the American life as we meet it today, with all its great or small imperfections, and the main concern is to get on as quickly as possible with the business of living. This is how America grew in the nineteenth century, headstrong, deliberately unsystematic in philosophy, simply making the best of a new, raw country. Everything in Howard's play is designed for the easy sympathy of the audience. Tony, the cuckolded husband, is extremely likeable. He has all of the charming, winning characteristics of the simple minded, good hearted man of the earth. How could an audience fail to support (or sympathize) with his eventual generosity in pardoning Amy and Joe? It is, obviously, what the audience would want for themselves. Most of all, it all adds up to excellent theater—combinations of moving realism and warming humor, and throughout, ample evidences of Howard's earnest sincerity. Only later, out of the theater, did the morally armed critics and church defenders begin to frame the expected opposition. The battle for theater freedom, however, had been already won on the only field that really mattered—the stage.

III   *The Writers' Craft*

Generally, Howard is thought of as a traditionalist in playwriting. Certainly in the company of O'Neill, Elmer Rice, and Thornton Wilder, there are no real pyrotechnics or daring stage innovations. In a 1925 interview, Howard labeled himself as an "artistic conservative," admittedly uninterested in contemporary expressionistic and impressionistic devices, his interest being people not people as ideas.[4] In late October, 1925, Howard sat down to write a preface to the unsuccessful *Lucky Sam McCarver.* He wrote at length in a delightful combination of bitterness, humor, and seriousness about the play's failure (with "the crash of critical crockery . . . still loud in my ears") and, most importantly, about the place of the dramatist in theater. The essay becomes Howard's major statement on the old argument of who matters more in theater, the writer or the actor. "For me," Howard pronounces quite bluntly, "the actor is the only theatrical element who matters a tinker's damn." All the other elements currently in theater (directors, scene-designers, costumers, even critics and electricians, as well as dramatists) are being talked of as more important than actors—and that Howard violently disagrees with. "Of all those concerned in the production of a play, only the actor utilizes his talents to the fullest." The others, Howard maintains, seem borrowed from elsewhere; ". . . the dramatist . . . is but a vicarious actor who happens to write well enough to be useful to real actors. Set him up among real literary men and he cuts a sorry figure" ("Preface," pp. xiv, xv).

The approach in these remarks seems to be fundamentally a defense of actors "at all costs," even at the expense of the dramatists. There is the feeling that in his enthusiasm for the actor's cause, Howard gets characteristically carried away and begins rather unevenly to rationalize a corresponding delimitation of the dramatist. He builds a case, certainly, but the well intentioned sincerity still seems doubtful. There is also the inclination to believe that the serious critical setback at this time with the new play quite naturally brings out the seemingly "logical" self-accusations of a dramatist among all other misunderstood dramatists. Part of the argument is that the great writers have never taken playwriting seriously, and that those who tried

(Tolstoy, Shelley, Browning) failed because they "offered the theatre literature and nothing else." All of this is true enough, but still overly simplified since there are so many non-literary factors that kept the gulf between the best men of letters and the theater in the nineteenth century. The basic argument here continues as essentially a showman's defense of the legitimate stage. The dramatist's function, Howard doggedly maintains, "none the less, is to serve actors, and the real merit of any play lies in the depth and scope of its acting parts far more than in its story or writing or idea content. The better, the more profoundly the dramatist writes, of course, the better he will serve actors, and that is his *raison d'être*. Audiences do not go to the theater to hear plays but to see them. No matter how beautiful the writing of a play may be, no matter how profound or original or true an idea it may contain, it cannot be a good play (let alone a great one) unless it allows actors to give an audience a satisfactory exhibition of their art" ("Preface," p. xvii).

In 1927 at the graduation exercises at the American Academy of Dramatic Arts in New York, Howard reemphasized his famous dictum that plays were essentially for actors. He introduced the topic (long familiar among his associates) by comparing the novelist and the playwright. He admitted that it was difficult to find the mind for doing plays although he certainly granted that a novel seems even more difficult. "I define the playwright's mind as the mind of a man who would rather see his story acted than write it out." The writer, he continued, becomes dependent on the actor. This is proven by the great playwrights (Shakespeare, Molière, Ibsen) being "house dramatists to a theatrical troupe." The actor fills out the little that the writer gives; the actor makes the part "into what the author would have written about that character had he written a novel instead of a play." In summation, then, "Plays are for actors . . . and to the art of acting the writing of plays is the secondary, subsidiary, and assistant thing."[5]

In effect, the above is a rather startling denigration of the playwrights' usually central role in theatrical productions. Friends thought the view was essentially derived from his actress wife, Clare Eames. There is no doubt that the heavy reliance on interpreters is in keeping with his fortunate association with a few excellent actors. At times, the list reads almost like a Howard road company: Katherine Cornell (two plays); Pauline Lord (three); Margalo Gillmore (two); Laura Hope Crews (two); Ethel Barrymore (one); and, of course, Clare Eames (four).[6] Generally, writing specifically for one actor (as Howard often does) is usually suspect in higher critical circles. The tailoring of characterizations can have an obviously limiting effect. Whatever constraints the practice may have had on his writing, he evidently welcomed it. Thus, the frequent frank admissions that the playwright is really subservient to the actor—implying, of course, the best and most professional actor. In 1930 John Mason Brown summarized the effects of such an approach to theater.

As actors' plays that are useful even before they are truthful or personal, Mr. Howard's scripts take their style not so much from what he has done in them as from what he has given others to do in them. To be sure, they are not vehicles in the old or tawdry sense of the word, because just as they are too intelligent and too individual for that so also are they too generous in the manner in which they distribute their acting honors. But vehicular they are in spite of that, smudged intentionally with stardust and skilfully fitted to the modern actor's range by a man who is so willing to grant preëminence to his players that he proudly admits "the best that any dramatist can hope is that his play may be a worthy vehicle." Mr. Howard's plays are vehicles, the worthy vehicles of realism, written as "shows" rather than as plays by a man who revels in the joys that the game of showmanship holds for its contestants. Hence it is that they are almost gleeful in the manner in which they submit truth to a double exposure, displaying the truth as Mr. Howard sees it at one and the same time that they are displaying it as he has enlarged it to embrace an acting opportunity.[7]

Howard seems to be following the earlier theories of Augustin Daly, Daniel Frohman, and particularly, Bronson Howard (no relation). Bronson Howard in his *The Autobiography of a Play* (1886) had little regard for literary values, and thought of a play as a stage production only. In addition, both Howards emphasize the "satisfactory" ending which pleases the audience. To Sidney Howard, the playwright Ferenc Molnar is a model to emulate. He wrote for actors, even in the smallest roles; and, most of all, he was not affected by the modern theater's "subservience to the alleged intelligentsia." To Molnar the theater is a place of "magical entertainment, a place in which the true poetry of the heart strings and the impulse to laugh are more essential than the ambition to think. . . ."[8] These are familiar Howard characteristics as a playwright—sincerity, sentiment, humor, and general good sense. Howard's habits during the rehearsals of his plays are also indications of the lesser position he holds for the script. He does not consider his words sacrosanct and is ready to change anything to make his "magical entertainment" work. An interviewer reported that "at rehearsal Howard is in his workshop. He writes, rewrites, cuts, and transposes as the rehearsal proceeds."[9] As Brooks Atkinson pointed out, in summarizing his praise for the engaging characters in *They Knew What They Wanted*, "They are products of Mr. Howard's instinct for the truth of other people and of his own modesty. He did not impose himself on his characters."[10]

IV *Final Estimate*

Howard's productivity has always been a source of amazement. Twenty-seven plays written for Broadway and all produced, over a peiod of eighteen years, 1921–1939. Add to this thirteen screenplays in the 1930's and we have a writer, who if nothing else, is a complete writing professional in the old sense. In 1948 there was some recognition of these facts in a poll of five-hundred actors, critics, playwrights, producers, and directors of both stage and screen. Howard was ranked eighth among the playwrights and fifth among the screen writers.[11] Of course, if monetary standing counts for anything, he was also the highest paid screen writer in Hollywood. The twenty-seven New York plays include thirteen original works, two of which are collaborations—*Bewitched* with Edward Sheldon and *Salvation* with Charles MacArthur. Even though *Yellow Jack* is listed as "with Paul de Kruif," everyone admits (including de Kruif) that the play is entirely Howard's. The other fourteen plays include nine translations (mostly hack work) and five adaptations, *The Late Christopher Bean, Dodsworth, Paths of Glory, Lute Song,* and *Ode to Liberty*—some of these easily among the best of Howard.

It is not uncommon to find the critics accounting for Howard's long and wide range of subjects on the basis of his concerns for the immediate and the concrete. Unlike deeper writers such as O'Neill and Wilder, Howard draws inspiration from the concrete situation. The remarkable effectiveness of so many of his plays, according to Joseph Wood Krutch, "has been due to the fact that they were less comments on contemporary life than presentations of it. One never knows what Mr. Howard is going to say. With him, one sometimes feels, a conviction is an enthusiasm and, like any other enthusiasm, likely to disappear as soon as it has emerged."[12] Such a directness toward life, toward experience is a fundamental Howard trait; it is clearly behind all the zealous acts of a busy life. It is the animating force of Howard's fictional women.

What is often, then, unusual in Howard's career is the sheer variety of convictions, as Krutch points out. Consistency, in itself, means little. For example, politically, Howard seems generally to be an idealist: witness the headlong rush to the battlefields in 1916. No one could doubt his Americanism. However, in 1932 in the depths of the Depression, he caused a mild sensation by coming out in support of William Z. Foster, Communist candidate for the presidency. He announced "he would campaign on behalf of the Intellectuals Committee for Foster, because he was fed up with the impotence and bungling of the two old parties."[13] Considering the dire predicament of our economic and social life during these years, such announcements seem less radical and more understandable from the viewpoint of forty years later. To Howard and other prominent intellectuals (Edmund Wilson, John Dos Passos, and many others) almost any political system which offered an immediate answer to the Depression deserved consideration. And yet, another characteristic inconsistency in the same year: Howard helped organize the radical Willard Straight Post of the American Legion which fought the parent organization on the issue of veterans' bonuses. The chapter took the position that recipients of the bonuses were "unpatriotic" and "disloyal." (Although their charter was canceled, they brought suit, won, and were readmitted.) What do these events tell us? According to Krutch, they completely characterize the essential Howard:

Together they give you the picture of a man who loves a row, or, rather, who loves a joyous participation in dramatic events. That also is the man who writes the plays. In them the clash of creeds and temperaments interests him for its own sake. He can take sides enthusiastically but he can also change them. He is, whether he knows it or not, pretty certain to be on the side most likely to precipitate a dramatic crisis and pretty likely, in his plays, to see to it that one takes place. Being also a man of intelligence, his attitude is usually intelligible and his crises significant. But it is the happening which interests him and the happening which interests his audience.[14]

Thus the numerous braveries of his indomitable heroines fighting their good fight against unfair (but always interesting) odds. Nearly impossible idealists they may be (as Sara in *The Ghost of Yankee Doodle*), but they speak their piece nevertheless. At times we well recognize the undeniable theatrical effects of strong words strongly spoken even when the issues themselves may be a bit muddled. A high excitement is always good theater. Howard himself was never above speaking plainly and bluntly, particularly when basic human issues were involved. In 1937 the Reich Theater Chamber in Germany was considering a production of *Dodsworth*. They wrote to Howard and Lewis that they "would need evidence of the dramatists' Aryan descent" before they could proceed. "Howard and Lewis, in a joint letter, protested that they could not provide that evidence."

. . . who knows what ancestors we may have had in the last few hundred years? We really are as ignorant of them as even Hitler of his.

In answering please use our proper legal names: Sidney Horowitz, Sinclair Levy.

Yours sincerely,
Sidney Howard and *Sinclair Lewis*[15]

Howard was among the first to admit that he was not a great dramatist, certainly not "the man for all the ages," as we sometimes say about the very greatest of literary talents. In a letter of 1929, disturbed about his divorce and doubtful about his abilities, he wrote to Barrett Clark: "I can't get off my track even if I had some exalted vision of my talents and wanted to do so, because I am and shall always be an earthbound pragmatic stoic without any aptitude for the empyrean" (Clark, p. 209). Words to this effect can be found throughout his correspondence. Evidently, he was never to be plagued by misguided notions of how great his talent was; fundamentally, he was content, in his own vigorous, square-jawed way, to stay firmly on his own limited ground. Numerous subjects were, seemingly, always ready at hand, and they were treatable in that same "earthbound pragmatic" way that had made *They Knew What They Wanted* such a success. Walter Meserve sums up: "Whereas O'Neill searched for an understanding of self throughout his plays, Howard assumed a knowledge and an identification, and on a social rather than a philosophical level dramatized the attempted romantic escape of the self from all that was confining."[16] Howard has the comfort of the settled conscience. His plays present reality rather than provoking it. He is not the lost writer gloriously trying to find himself in his plays.

It is sensible then to appraise Howard in the same reasonable way of mild expectations. In his own time his virtues were apparent enough—the good craftsman, the appropriate language, the obvious sincerity—to win him a popular following and respectable critical acceptance. There should be no difficulty in extending such particular virtues into lasting values in the history of American dramatic literature. There are, after all, such a small number of influential dramatists at any time, and surely Howard holds his place in this company. "Writing a play," Howard once said, "is just getting excited enough about a character to fasten him down on paper." The evidence in the major plays brings back to life again the quick zeal and boyish enthusiasms of a healthful personality. In his day, Howard stirred up a good deal of theatrical excitement on Broadway. "No one," for example, was "bored by *The Silver Cord*," wrote Brooks Atkinson, "although some people were frightened." And that in the final analysis is a fair compliment for the energetic Mr. Howard.[17]

Notes and References

Preface

1. Joseph Wood Krutch, "Sidney Howard, Storyteller," *Theatre Arts*, 41 (February, 1957), 91.
2. *Time*, 23 (March 19, 1934), 36.
3. Alan Downer, *Dictionary of American Biography*, Supplement II, 22 (1958), 324.
4. Letter to Mrs. John Howard, January 5, 1917, Sidney Coe Howard Collection, University of California, Berkeley.
5. Glenn Hughes, *A History of the American Theatre, 1700–1950* (London: Samuel French, 1951), p. 397.
6. Walter J. Meserve, "Sidney Howard and the Social Drama of the Twenties," *Modern Drama*, 6 (December, 1963), 256.

Chapter One

1. Letter to Barrett Clark in Barrett H. Clark. *Intimate Portraits* (Port Washington, New York: Kennikat Press [1951], rpt. 1970), p. 212. (Hereafter cited as Clark.) There were six children in all, four from the father's previous marriage. Howard was next to the youngest.
2. George Pierce Baker (1866–1935) taught at Harvard for thirty-seven years; he began to formulate his views on American theater in the early 1900's, and by 1905 had begun the famous English 47 course, The Technique of the Drama. The course was a combination of lectures and practice and by 1913 included the "47 Workshop." The first play professionally produced from the course was Edward Sheldon's *Salvation Nell* (1907) at the Providence Opera House. Starring Mrs. Fiske, the play's success gave the course national prestige. The new Yale theater drew Baker away in 1925 until his retirement in 1933. See Wisner Payne Kinne, *G. P. Baker and the American Theatre* (Cambridge: The Harvard Press, 1954).
3. Sidney Howard, "George Pierce Baker of Harvard and Yale," New York *Times* (February 5, 1933), sec. ix, p. 3.
4. Letter to Mrs. John Howard, n.d. [c. 1916], Howard Collection, Berkeley.

147

5. Letter to Mrs. John Howard, n.d. [c. 1915], Howard Collection, Berkeley.

6. Letter to Mrs. John Howard, October 21, 1916, Howard Collection, Berkeley.

7. Sidney Howard, "The Stars in Their Courses," *Collier's*, 66 (November 6, 1920), 5.

8. Evidently, Howard possessed a sufficient knowledge of French, Hungarian, and Italian. According to Charles Scott, Howard could speak French, Italian, some Spanish and a little German. See his dissertation, "Sidney Howard," Ph.D., Yale, 1963, p. 52.

9. Letter to Mrs. Jean McDuffie, July 28, 1917, Howard Collection, Berkeley.

10. Sidney Howard "flew in the Lorraine defensive sector and the St. Michel and Meuse Argonne offensives." He was terminated as a Captain, Aviation Section. From a "Military History of Sidney Howard," April 24, 1956, Department of the Army.

11. Nazimova had disagreed with the staging; nevertheless Sidney Howard was paid for his work. Plans included production at the Greek Theater, Berkeley.

12. Sidney Howard, "The Colyer Trial Opens," *The Survey*, 44 (April 17, 1920), 105: "In Judge Anderson's Court," *The Survey*, 44 (May 1, 1920), 182–84; "Judge Anderson's Decision," *The Survey*, 44 (July 3, 1920), 489–90.

13. Sidney Howard and Robert Dunn, "The Labor Spy," *The New Republic*, 25 (February 16, 23, 1921); 26 (March 1, 9, 16, 23, 30, 1921). Reprinted as *The Labor Spy* (New York: Republic Publishing Co., 1924) with three-fourths additional material. Thirty thousand copies of the original had been printed earlier in pamphlet form to meet the demand. The research bureau was headed by Dr. Richard C. Cabot, Professor of Social Ethics at Harvard.

14. Sidney Howard, "The Inside Story of Dope in This Country," *Hearst's International*, 43 (February, March, April, May, June, 1923), 44 (July 1923); "Stock Swindlings: The Great Modern Shell Game," *Hearst's International*, 44 (October, 1923), 18; "Oil Crooks," *Hearst's International*, 44 (November, 1923), 31.

15. Sidney Howard, "Our Professional Patriots," *The New Republic* (August 20, September 3, 10, 17, 24, 1924).

16. Sidney Howard and John Hearley, *Professional Patriots*, ed. Norman Hapgood (New York: Albert and Charles Boni, 1927).

17. *Professional Patriots*, p. 3.

18. Among these, three were to see production: *Casanova* (1923), a translation of the play of the same name by Lorenzo de Azertis;

Sancho Panza (1923), an adaptation of a play by Melchoir Lengyel; and *S. S. Tenacity* (1922), a translation of a play by Charles Vildrac.

19. The set design appeared in the International Exposition at Amsterdam in 1930, where Gordon Craig judged it "the most original drawing sent by an American." *Theatre Guild Magazine*, 8 (November, 1930), 19.

20. Barrett H. Clark and George Freedly, eds. *A History of Modern Drama* (New York: D. Appleton-Century Co., 1947), p. 683.

21. Laurence Langer, *The Magic Curtain* (New York: Dutton, 1951), p. 218.

22. Letter to Elizabeth Sergeant, September 10, 1921, Howard Collection, Berkeley.

23. S. Marion Tucker, *Modern Continental Plays* (New York: Harper & Bros., 1929), p. 757.

24. Robert Littell, *Theatre Arts*, 8 (December, 1924), 803.

25. Stephen Vincent Benct, "Is Costume Drama Dead?" *The Bookman*, 60 (December, 1924), 482.

26. Sidney Howard, *Three Flights Up* (New York: Scribner's, 1924).

27. John Temple, "Sidney Howard: A Biographical Sketch," *Asides*, #2 (Stanford Univ. Dramatists Alliance, 1941), p. 32.

28. Burns Mantle, "Law Takes a Hand," New York *News* (February 14, 1925) and "Play Juries Acquit Two Shows as Clean," New York *Times* (March 14, 1925), p. 15. For the Will Hays issue see New York *Times* (July 23, 1925), p. 22 and New York *Times* (July 24, 1925), p. 12. *They Knew What They Wanted* was eventually filmed in 1928 as *The Secret Hour*.

29. Howard appeared before the committee between March 9 and 19, 1927. "Stage Censorship Plea Impresses Legislators," New York *Times* (March 10, 1927), p. 1; "Howard Names State Foes," New York *Times* (March 16, 1927), pp. 8, 12. Addressing the graduating class at the American Academy of Dramatic Arts on March 15, he gave similar views against censorship. New York *Times* (March 20, 1927), p. 4.

30. Translation of another Charles Vildrac play, *Michael Auclair*, 19 performances. Translation from Edmond Rostand, *The Last Night of Don Juan*, 16 performances. An "arrangement" of Ludwig Thoma's *Morality*, translated and adapted by Charles Recht in 1905, now entitled *Morals*, 40 performances. An original, *Lucky Sam McCarver*, 29 performances.

31. Montrose J. Moses considered the play one of Howard's most distinguished dramas. *Representative American Dramas* (Boston:

Little, Brown & Co., 1925), p. 669. Burns Mantle seriously considered it one of the ten best of the year. *The Best Plays of 1925–26,* ed. Burns Mantle (New York: Dodd, Mead & Co., 1926), p. 3.

32. Henry A. Adams. "Sidney Howard: A Critical Study," Unpublished Manuscript dated "New York City, March 19, 1940," p. 56, in the Howard Collection, Berkeley.

33. "The Homesick Ladies," *Scribner's Magazine* (April, 1929), p. 85.

34. *Salvation* (1928), a collaboration with Charles MacArthur, based on the evangelist Aimee S. MacPherson, 31 performances. *Olympia* (1928), translation of Ferenc Molnar, 39 performances. *Half Gods* (1929), 17 performances. *One, Two, Three* (1930), translation of a one-act play by Ferenc Molnar, 40 performances. *Marseilles* (1930), translation of *Marius* by Marcel Pagol, 16 performances.

35. The usual depression on reaching his forties. Howard feared he had overextended himself in plays and films; perhaps forty was the limit of his creative talent. *Diary,* June 9, 1931. Howard Collection, Berkeley.

36. Barrett H. Clark, "His Voice was American," *Theatre Arts* (April, 1949), p. 30.

37. *Diary,* December 19, 1930, Howard Collection, Berkeley. Also in 1931: "I am preparing for it [Wilson] with my head in a shelf of books some hours daily." (Clark, p. 217).

38. Fred B. Millett. *Contemporary American Authors* (London: George G. Harrap & Co., 1940), p. 402.

39. Howard even had a plan to help the young playwright *after* his initial failure on Broadway. He influenced John Golden to Award $5000 in fellowships through the Dramatist's Guild. The award committee included Frank Crowninshield, Golden, Burns Mantle, George Kaufman, and Howard. See Temple, *Asides,* p. 37.

40. Studios were acting as play producers in order to secure film rights to scripts at lower cost. The playwrights needed control over who the producers would be so that the studios could not take over and dictate that the writers do only plays suitable for films. New York *Times* (April 12, 1936), Sec. ix, p. 1.

41. Arthur Hobson Quinn, *A History of the American Drama From the Civil War to the Present Day,* II (London: Sir Isaac Pitman & Sons, 1937), p. 274.

42. New York *Times* (February 23, 1936), p. 3.

43. Incorporated as The Playwrights' Producing Company with six directors: Maxwell Anderson, S. N. Behrman, Sidney Howard,

Elmer Rice, Robert Sherwood, and attorney John Wharton. Each of the playwrights contributed $10,000 and an additional $50,000 was privately raised. The basic idea had been last suggested in 1929 by Rice to Anderson, Phillip Barry, and George Kelly, but with no success. John F. Wharton's *Life Among the Playwrights* (New York: New York *Times* Book Co., 1974), is a complete history of the company. See also Elmer Rice, *Minority Report* (New York: Simon and Schuster, 1963), pp. 374–76.

44. S. N. Behrman, *People in a Diary* (Boston: Little, Brown, 1972), pp. 213–17.

45. Rudy Behlmer, ed. *Memo from David O. Selznick* (New York: The Viking Press, 1972), p. 160.

46. Howard wrote in his Diary for March 4, 1939: "Peace and work and chopping trees." The family tradition seems to be continuing. Howard's son, Walter, manages the very active dairy farm today, and on my visit with him in June, 1974, was up to his elbows with spring mud.

47. Dorothy Thompson, "On the Record," New York *Herald-Tribune* (August 28, 1939), p. 14.

Chapter Two

1. At Harvard, Hume had done everything in the first 47 Workshop production in 1912: acted the leading role, designed the sets, did the lights and costumes. See Cecil Hinkel, "An Analysis and Evaluation of the 47 Workshop of George Pierce Baker," Ph.D. Dissertation. (Ohio State University, 1959, pp. 174, 179).

2. The pageant was done again as *The Quest* at Santa Barbara in July, 1920, and at the Greek Theater, Berkeley, in August, 1920. See Mary Morris, *The Drama*, 11 (November, 1920), 43.

3. John Temple, "Sidney Howard: A Biographical Sketch and Bibliography," *Asides*, p. 33 Also, see New York *Times* (April 14, 1924), p. 9 and (April 20, 1924), p. 8.

4. *Swords* opened in New York on September 1, 1921, for thirty-six performances, starring Clare Eames as Fiamma.

5. Kenneth McGowan, "Year's End," *Theatre Arts Monthly*, 6 (January, 1922), 8.

6. Ludwig Lewisohn, "Drama: Homespun and Brocade," *The Nation*, 113 (September 21, 1921), 324. See also Alexander Woolcott, New York *Times* (September 2, 1921), p. 9; and Robert Benchley, *Life*, 78 (September 22, 1921), 18.

7. *Bewitched* opened in New York on October 1, 1924, for

twenty-nine performances, starring Glen Anders and Florence Eldridge.

8. Eric W. Barnes, *The Man Who Lived Twice* (New York: Scribner's 1956), pp. 147–48.

9. Richard Dana Skinner, "Glory and Claptrap," *The Independent*, 113 (November 15, 1924), 403. Heywood Broun, New York *World* (October 2, 1924).

10. *S. S. Tenacity* opened in New York on January 2, 1922, for sixty-seven performances, starring Augustin Duncan as Hidoux. *Michael Auclair* opened in New York on March 4, 1925, for nineteen performances, at the new Provincetown Playhouse, produced by Robert Edmond Jones, Kenneth Macgowan, and Eugene O'Neill. Howard's enthusiasm for the new company was genuine: (in a letter to Macgowan) "As to cash, you fix whatever you can afford to pay and stick my name on as translator and that's all." Letter dated June 15, 1924, as Appendix in Bernard H. Craven, "Sidney Howard, The Man and His Plays," M.A. Thesis, UCLA, 1950, p. 102.

11. Joseph Wood Krutch, *The Nation,* 120 (March 25, 1925), 334. See also, Gilbert Gabriel, New York *Telegram* (March 7, 1925).

12. The manuscript of *Jacob Ely* is in the Howard Collection, Berkeley.

13. Sidney Howard, "The Stars in Their Courses," *Collier's*, 66 (November 6, 1920).

14. Sidney Howard, "A Likeness of Elizabeth," *McCall's*, 52 (November, 1924). Included in Howard's collection, *Three Flights Up* (New York: Scribner's, 1924).

15. Sidney Howard, "Transatlantic," *Three Flights Up* (New York: Scribner's 1924).

16. Sidney Howard, "Mrs. Vietch: A Segment of Biography," *Three Flights Up* (New York: Scribner's, 1924).

17. Sidney Howard, "The God They Left Behind Them," *Three Flights Up* (New York: Scribner's, 1924).

18. Janet A. Smith, ed. *Henry James & Robert Louis Stevenson* (London: Rupert Hart-Davis, 1948), pp. 37, 157.

19. Sidney Howard, "Such Women as Ellen Steele," *Scribner's Magazine*, 77 (January, 1925).

20. Sidney Howard, "The Homesick Ladies," *Scribner's Magazine,* 85 (April, 1929), 379–94. Included in Blanche Colton Williams, ed. *O. Henry Memorial Award Prize Stories of 1929* (New York: Doubleday, Doran & Co., 1930), pp. 29–51. First prize won by Dorothy Parker for "Big Blonde."

21. Probably modeled after Howard's summer retreat at Wiscasset, Maine, in the 1920's.

Chapter Three

1. *They Knew What They Wanted* opened in New York on November 24, 1924, for 414 performances. The cast included Richard Bennett as Tony, Pauline Lord as Amy, and Glen Anders as Joe. It was awarded the Pulitzer Prize, and made into a film three times. In 1956 Frank Loesser turned the play into a successful musical, *The Most Happy Fella*, which ran for two years.

2. Willis Coleman, "He Knew What He Wanted," *Theatre Magazine*, 42 (September, 1925), 10.

3. Sidney Howard, "Preface," *They Knew What They Wanted*, (New York: Doubleday, Page & Co., 1925), p. xiii. Howard needed his own tolerance toward a charge of plagiarism brought in 1927. The case, however, was dismissed when Barrett Clark gave the long list of literary parallels common in the fifteenth and sixteenth centuries, all derived from the same Tristran and Yseult legend. (New York *Times*, April 26 and 27, 1927), pp. 33 and 10.

4. I.W.W.—International Workers of the World. Members were derogatorily called, "Wobblies," the name for Joe that Tony freely uses.

5. New York *World* (November 25, 1924), p. 15.

6. New York *Evening Sun* (November 25, 1924), p. 24.

7. New York *Herald Tribune* (November 25, 1924), p. 17.

8. *American Mercury*, 4 (January, 1925), 121.

9. Reginald Hargreaves, *Theatre World* [London] 3 (June, 1926), 51. The London production featured Tallulah Bankhead as Amy, Glen Anders as Joe, and Sam Livesey as Tony.

10. *Theatre World* [London] (July, 1926), p. 55.

11. Arthur Hornblow, *Theatre Magazine*, 41 (February, 1925), 19.

12. Arthur Hornblow, *Theatre Magazine*, 42 (July, 1925), 7. The Pulitzer instructions were subsequently altered to remove the moral conditions. The other chief contender for the prize, *What Price Glory*, probably lost out because of its rougher, more censorable language. John Toohey, *A History of the Pulitzer Prize Plays* (New York: The Citadel Press, 1967), p. 44. Howard himself considered *What Price Glory* the better play. *Stage Magazine* (February, 1935), p. 21.

13. Both playwrights deny that the similarity of the two plays is anything more than a coincidence. *They Knew What They Wanted*

opened in New York November 24, 1924; *Desire Under the Elms,* November 11, 1924.

14. *American Drama Since 1918.* (London: Thames and Hudson, 1957), pp. 49, 50.

Chapter Four

1. *Lucky Sam McCarver* opened in New York on October 21, 1925, for twenty-nine performances. The cast included John Cromwell as Sam and Clare Eames as Carlotta Ashe. The play is one of two that Howard directed, the other being *Ode to Liberty* (1934).

2. Sidney Howard, "Preface" to *Lucky Sam McCarver* (New York: Charles Scribner's Sons, 1926), p. xiv.

3. Montrose J. Moses, *Representative American Dramas* (Boston: Little, Brown & Co., 1925), p. 669.

4. Burns Mantle, *The Best Plays of 1925–26,* p. 3.

5. John Mason Brown, *Upstage* (New York: W. W. Norton, 1930), p. 59.

6. *Ned McCobb's Daughter* opened in New York on November 22, 1926 (a month before *The Silver Cord*) for 132 performances, making it the fifth most successful play. The cast included Clare Eames as Carrie, Margalo Gillmore as Jenny, Alfred Lunt as Babe, Earle Larrimore as George, Edward G. Robinson as Grover, and Morris Carnovsky as the Second Federal Man. Gillmore and Larrimore appeared in both plays.

7. Robert Coleman, "Howard's Comedy Sordid," New York *Daily Mirror* (December 3, 1926), p. 21.

8. Charles Brackett, *New Yorker,* 2 (December 11, 1926), 39.

9. Joseph Wood Krutch, *The Nation,* 73 (December 29, 1926), 697.

10. John Mason Brown "The Gaunt of Style," *Theatre Arts Monthly,* 11 (February, 1927), 96.

11. Glenn Hughes, *A History of the American Theatre* (London: Samuel French, 1951) p. 397.

12. *The Silver Cord* opened in New York on December 20, 1926, for 112 performances, making it the sixth most successful play. The New York cast included Margalo Gillmore as Hester, Eliot Cabot as David, Elizabeth Risdon as Christina, Earle Larrimore as Robert, and Laura Hope Crews as Mrs. Phelps. Clare Eames played Christina, Brian Aherne, David, and Lillian Braithwaite, Mrs. Phelps in the London production beginning September 13, 1927.

13. Joseph Wood Krutch, *The Nation,* 137 (September 13, 1933), 294.

14. Arthur Hornblow, *Theatre Magazine*, 45 (February, 1927), 58.

15. *Ibid.*

16. The Scribner text of 1927 has these lines. Other texts have the following, which appear to be from the acting version: "And you can use your imagination about the rest." A stage production that I saw at M.I.T. used the latter, which seemed equally effective, but of course, without the possibility or intrigue of stage censorship.

17. Stark, Young, *Immortal Shadows* (New York: Scribner's, 1948), p. 77. Collected Broadway reviews.

18. Desmond, McCarthy, *Drama* (London: Putnam, 1940), p. 221. The *New Statesman* reviews, 1913–1935.

19. *The New Republic* (February 9, 1927), 49: 328.

20. Letter to Mrs. Jean McDuffie, June 30, 1926, Howard Collection, Berkeley.

21. *Half Gods* opened in New York on December 21, 1929 for only 17 performances, making it the least successful of all his plays. (Only *Marseilles* [1930], a translation from Marcel Pagnol, did worse at 16.) The cast included Donn Cook as Stephen Ferrier, Mayo Methot as Hope Ferrier, Walter Regan as Rush Bigelow, Walter Walker as Judge Sturgis, Dorothy Sands as Helena Grey, and Edward Reese as Dr. Mannering.

22. Joseph Wood Krutch, "Drama: A Peevish Play," *The Nation* (January 8, 1930) p. 52.

23. John Hutchens, *Theatre Arts Monthly*, 14 (February, 1930), 109.

Chapter Five

1. *Lute Song* was first presented on September 1, 1930 at the Berkshire Playhouse, Stockbridge, Massachusetts. The New York production did not come about until February 6, 1946, for a run of 142 performances. Produced by Michael Myerberg at a relatively high cost, the "pageant-spectacle" featured the most prominent stage people: John Houseman, director; Robert Edmond Jones, designer; and music by Raymond Scott. The cast included Mary Martin as Tchao-Ou-Niang, Yul Brynner as Tsai-Yong, Augustin Duncan as Tsai, Mildred Dunnock as Mme. Tsai, and Clarence Derwent as the Manager and Tschang.

2. "On the Trail of a Chinese Script," New York *Times* (February 3, 1946).

3. Ward Morehouse, The New York *Sun* (February 7, 1946). All the critics agreed that it was the designer's show, Robert Edmond Jones at his best. The Mary Martin songs, "Mountain High, Valley

Low," and "Monkey See, Monkey Do," had a sizeable, popular following.

4. John Chapman, *Daily News* (February 7, 1946), p. 15.

5. Louis Kronenberger, *PM* (February 8, 1946), p. 12.

6. *The Late Christopher Bean*, first titled, "The Muse of All Work," is an adaptation of *Prenez Garde à la Peinture* by René Fauchois, which opened in Paris, March, 1932. Another version of the French play was written by Emlyn Williams for the English stage in 1933. See *Famous Plays of 1933* (London: Victor Gollancz Ltd., 1933). The Howard play ran for 224 performances, making it the third most successful. The cast included Walter Connolly as Dr. Haggett, Beulah Bondi as Mrs. Haggett, and Pauline Lord as Abby.

7. Bernard H. Craven, "Sidney Howard, The Man and His Plays," M.A. Thesis, UCLA, 1950, p. 67. An excellent detailed comparison of the three plays.

8. Herschel Williams, *Theatre Arts Monthly*, 17 (January, 1933), 18.

9. Richard Dana Skinner, *Commonweal*, 17 (March 15, 1933), 17.

10. Joseph Wood Krutch, *The American Drama Since 1918* (London: Thames & Hudson, 1957), p. 57.

11. *Alien Corn* opened in New York on February 20, 1933 for 96 performances. The cast included Katherine Cornell as Elsa, Luther Adler as Julian, and James Rennie as Harry Conway.

12. Joseph Wood Krutch, *The Nation*, 136 (March 15, 1933), 299.

13. Brooks Atkinson, New York *Times* (February 21, 1933), p. 17.

14. Morton Eustis, *Theatre Arts Monthly*, 17 (May, 1933), 342.

15. *Commonweal*, 17 (March 15, 1933), 553.

16. The novel, *Dodsworth*, was published in 1929. The adaptation, *Dodsworth*, opened in New York on February 24, 1934, for 278 performances. Financially, it was Howard's greatest success. The cast included Walter Huston as Sam Dodsworth, Fay Bainter as Fran Dodsworth, Nan Sunderland as Mrs. Edith Cortright, John Williams as Major Clyde Lockert, Kent Smith as Baron Kurt von Obersdorf, and Maria Ouspenskaya as the Baroness von Obersdorf.

17. It is interesting to compare these final lines with the Howard script of *Gone With The Wind* (1939). The same kind of question is put by Scarlett to Rhett: What to do? The famous answer ("Frankly, my dear, I don't give a damn!") is not really Sam Dodsworth's style.

18. Sidney Howard, "A Postscript on Dramatization," *Dodsworth* (New York: Harcourt, Brace & Co., 1934), p. vii.

19. Cited in Mark Schorer, *Sinclair Lewis* (New York: McGraw-Hill Book Co., 1961), p. 576.

20. Sinclair Lewis, "The Art of Dramatization," *Dodsworth* (New York: Harcourt, Brace & Co., 1934), p. lxiii.

21. Lewis, p. lxvi.

22. Sidney Howard, "A Postscript on Dramatization," p. xvi.

23. Robert Garland, New York *World-Telegram* (February 26, 1934).

24. Arthur Hobson Quinn, *A History of the American Drama From the Civil War to the Present Day* (London: Pitman & Sons, 1937), II, p. 274.

25. Hiram Motherwell, "Sam Dodsworth Sees the World," *The Stage*, 11 (March, 1934), 14.

Chapter Six

1. *Yellow Jack* opened in New York on March 6, 1934 for seventy-nine performances. The cast included James Stewart as O'Hara, Myron McCormick as Brinkerhof, Sam Levene as Busch, John Miltern as Walter Reed, Barton MacLane as James Carroll, and Edward Cianneli as Agramonte.

2. Paul de Kruif, "Backstage with 'Yellow Jack,'" *Stage* (June, 1938), p. 28.

3. New York *Herald Tribune* (March 7, 1934), p. 15.

4. *Stage* (April, 1934), pp. 8, 10.

5. Barrett Clark, "His Voice was American," *Theatre Arts* (April, 1949), p. 30.

6. John Mason Brown, *Theatre Arts Monthly* (March 10, 1934), p. 8.

7. Joseph Wood Krutch, *The Nation*, 138 (March 21, 1934), 340.

8. *Paths of Glory*, an adaptation of the novel by the same name by Humphrey Cobb, opened in New York on September 26, 1935, for 23 performances. The cast included Jack Rosleigh as General Assolant, Edgar Barrier as Capt. Renouart, Jerome Cowan as Ferol, George Tobias as Meyer, William Harrigan as Didier, and Myron McCormick as Langlois. Stanley Kubrick in 1957 made the story into a successful film.

9. Quinn, *A History of the American Drama From the Civil War to the Present Day*, II, p. 275.

10. Sidney Howard, "A Foreword for All College Theatres and for All Amateurs of Military Age," *Paths of Glory* (New York: Samuel French, 1935), p. xiii.

11. *Ibid.*, p. ix.

12. Edith Isaacs, *Theatre Arts*, 19 (November, 1935), 814.

13. George Jean Nathan, *Vanity Fair*, 45 (December, 1935), 45.

14. Clifton Fadiman, "Bypaths of Glory," *Stage*, 13 (November. 1935), p. 46.

15. Sidney Howard, "Foreword," *Paths of Glory*, p. xvi.

16. Lee Mitchell, "The Tributary Theatre," *Theatre Arts*, 20 (January, 1936), 75.

17. *The Ghost of Yankee Doodle* opened in New York on October 28, 1937, for forty-eight performances. The cast included Ethel Barrymore as Sara Garrison, Frank Conroy as John Garrison, Richard Carlson as Martin Holme, Dudley Digges as Clevenger, and Eliot Cabot as Rudi Garrison.

18. Sidney Howard, "Waking, Not Walking, the Ghost," New York *Times* (November 21, 1937), ix, p. 1.

19. George Jean Nathan, "A-Riding On a Phony," *Newsweek*, 10 (December 6, 1937), 32.

20. Edith Isaacs, *Theatre Arts*, 22 (January, 1938), 20.

21. Grenville Vernon, *Commonweal*, 27 (December 10, 1937), 191.

22. *Madam, Will You Walk?* had its tryout in Baltimore on November 13, 1939, and was withdrawn on November 17. The cast included George M. Cohan as Dr. Brightlee, Peggy Conklin as Mary, Keenan Wynn as Dockwiler, and Arthur Kennedy as Scupper. The first New York production was on December 1, 1953, for forty-two performances. The cast included Hume Cronyn (also co-director) as Dr. Brightlee, Jessica Tandy as Mary, Norman Lloyd (also co-director) as Dockwiler, and Robert Emmett as Scupper. A recent presentation of the play was a reading by Loyola Marymount University, Los Angeles, in April, 1977, with Howard's daughter, Jennifer, giving introductory remarks.

23. Clark, p. 30.

24. Wharton, p. 72.

25. Rice, p. 390.

26. *Ibid.*

27. Behrman, p. 219.

28. Wharton, pp. 72–73.

29. Behrman, p. 219.

30. Wharton, p. 74.

31. Michael Mok, "Sidney Howard Loves Nearly Everything Except Things Like Social Messages," New York *Post* (August 16, 1939).

32. Brooks Atkinson, New York *Times* (December 2, 1953), p. 17.

33. Harold Clurman, *The Nation*, 177 (December 19, 1953), 554.

34. Clark, p. 30.

35. See Robert Coleman, New York *Daily Mirror* (December 11, 1953). John Chapman, New York *Daily News* (December 9, 1953) called it "an unresolved fantasy" because the court scene with the Shavian elements resolved nothing. Richard Watts, Jr., New York *Post* (December 15, 1953) faulted George M. Cohan for giving up the play in its 1939 Baltimore tryout. Cohan complained he didn't know what Howard was writing about. "I think," wrote Watts, "that the eminent actor made a mistake."

36. Walter Kerr, New York *Herald Tribune* (December 3, 1953), p. 25.

Chapter Seven

1. Letter to Mrs. Jean McDuffie, Berkeley, January 15, 1929, Howard Collection, Berkeley. Howard's oldest daughter, Clare ("Jennifer") married Samuel Goldwyn's son.

2. New York *Times* (May 3, 1929, p. 23). In addition to the credited screen work, Howard worked on a number of others, including, *Madame Curie* (1936), *The Prisoner of Zenda* (1937), *The Real Glory* (1939), and *Northwest Passage* (1940).

3. Gertrude Stutzman, "Sidney Howard, Playwright and Personality," M.A. Thesis, University of Washington, 1947, p. 135.

4. "Sidney Howard Backs Lewis in Film Row," New York *Times* (February 23, 1936), p. 3.

5. Howard Collection, Berkeley.

6. Rudy Behlmer, ed. *Memo From David O. Selznick* (New York: The Viking Press, 1972), p. 62. Hereafter cited as *Selznick*.

7. Howard Collection, Berkeley.

8. Bob Thomas, *Selznick* (New York: Doubleday & Co., 1970), p. 146.

9. Fitzgerald was hired in January, 1939, for two weeks to do dialogue. He was unable to do a rewrite of the staircase scene. After being fired he confessed to Maxwell Perkins that no words but the author's were allowed—"as if it were Scripture." Thomas, *Selznick*, p. 146.

10. Selznick letter, January 25, 1939, to J. H. Whitney: "The Garrett script is infinitely better as to continuity and as to storytelling generally, but inferior to the Howard script as to each individual scene" (*Selznick*, pp. 188, 189).

11. Gavin Lambert, *GWTW: The Making of Gone With the Wind* (Boston: Atlantic-Little, Brown, 1973), p. 71.

12. Lambert, p. 94.

13. Thomas, p. 168.

14. Frank S. Nugent, New York *Times* (December 20, 1939), p. 31.

15. Nugent, p. 31.

16. Mordant Hall, New York *Times* (November 4, 1929), p. 28.

17. Mordant Hall, New York *Times* (December 8, 1931), p. 36.

18. Frank Nugent, New York *Times* (September 24, 1936), p. 29.

19. Letter to Mrs. Jean McDuffie, February 15, 1929, Howard Collection, Berkeley.

20. Sidney Howard, "Views of the Motion Picture Industry," New York *Times* (December 1, 1929), p. 8.

21. Sidney Howard, "Hollywood on the Slide," *The New Republic*, 72 (November 9, 1932), 350.

Chapter Eight

1. *Salvation,* a collaboration of Howard with Charles MacArthur, opened in New York on January 31, 1928, for thirty-one performances. The cast included Pauline Lord as Bethany, Osgood Perkins as the press agent Whittaker, George MacFarlane as Brady, and Helen Ware as Mrs. Jones. According to Joseph Wood Krutch, there is an artless blending of two styles: Whittaker, the cynical stage reporter, another Hildy Johnson as in MacArthur's *The Front Page*; and Bethany, melodramatically drawn in Howard's heroic style. "The Drama: Actors to the Rescue," *The Nation*, 76 (February 22, 1928), 220.

2. Joseph Wood Krutch, *American Drama Since 1918* (London: Thames & Hudson, 1957), p. 47.

3. Bronson Howard (no relation of Sidney Howard) in a lecture called "Autobiography of a Play" delivered at Harvard in 1886. *The Autobiography of a Play* (New York: Dramatic Museum of Columbia University, 1914), pp. 27, 28.

4. Interview with Willis Coleman, "He Knew What He Wanted," *Theatre Magazine*, 42 (September, 1925), 10.

5. "Sidney Howard Speaking," New York *Times* (March 20, 1927), Sec. 13, p. 4.

6. The Howard "road company"—actors and plays: Katherine Cornell: Elsa (*Alien Corn*), Henriette (*Casanova*); Pauline Lord: Abby (*Christopher Bean*), Amy (*They Knew What They Wanted*), Bethany (*Salvation*); Margalo Gillmore: Jenny (*Ned McCobb*), Hester (*The Silver Cord*); Laura Hope Crews, Mrs. Phelps (*The Silver Cord*), Princess Eugenia (*Olympia*); Ethel Barrymore: Sara (*Yankee Doodle*); Clare Eames: Christina (*The Silver Cord*), Carlotta (*Sam McCarver*), Carrie (*Ned McCobb*), Fiamma (*Swords*); Glen An-

ders: Joe (*They Knew What They Wanted*), Jimmie (*Bewitched*); Augustin Duncan: Hidoux (*S.S. Tenacity*).

7. John Mason Brown, *Upstage* (New York: W. W. Norton, 1930), p. 54.

8. Sidney Howard, Preface, *Olympia*, translation of the play by Ferenc Molnar (New York: Brentano's, 1928). The play opened in New York October 16, 1928, for thirty-nine performances. The cast included Lauro Hope Crews as Princess Eugenia, Fay Compton as Olympia, and Ian Hunter as Captain Kovacs.

9. New York *Times* (February 19, 1933).

10. Brooks Atkinson, *The Lively Years, 1920–1973* (New York: Association Press, 1973), p. 44.

11. "The Best Since '23," *Theatre Arts*, 32 (August-September, 1948), 63.

12. Krutch, p. 55.

13. Harold Clurman, *The Fervent Years* (London: Dennis Hobson, 1946), p. 121.

14. Krutch, p. 57.

15. Mark Schorer, *Sinclair Lewis* (New York: McGraw-Hill Book Co., 1961), p. 628.

16. Walter Meserve, "Sidney Howard and the Social Drama of the Twenties," *Modern Drama*, 6 (1963), 264.

17. Atkinson, p. 51.

Selected Bibliography

The major depository of Howard materials is the Bancroft Library of the University of California at Berkeley. The Sidney Coé Howard Collection is extensive (over 16 boxes and 22 cartons), and of great literary value. The large correspondence alone to the major playwrights and authors of the 1920's and 1930's provides revealing insights into the times. The Princeton University Scribner Archives houses 47 letters from Howard and 161 to him. The Yale University Library has Theatre Guild "Press Books" concerning *They Knew What They Wanted*, *The Silver Cord*, *Ned McCobb's Daughter*, and *The Ghost of Yankee Doodle*. The Theatre Collection of the New York Public Library has "Clipping Files," and "Press Books" for *Swords*, *Olympia*, *Lute Song*, *Marseilles*, *Alien Corn*, *Yellow Jack*, *The Late Christopher Bean*, *Dodsworth*, *Paths of Glory*, *Madam*, *Will You Walk?* and *Salvation*.

PRIMARY SOURCES

1. *Plays (and short stories)*. Plays are listed in the order of their first presentation—in brackets; stories are listed by publication.

"The Stars in Their Courses" (short story). *Colliers'*, 66 (November 6, 1920), p. 5.

Swords [1921]. New York: George H. Doran, 1921.

S.S. Tenacity [1922] (Translation of *Le Paquebôt Tenacité* by Charles Vildrac). In S. Marion Tucker (ed.), *Modern Continental Plays*. New York: Harper & Brothers, 1929.

Casanova [1923] (Translation of *Casanova* by Lorenzo de Azertis, psued. of Lorand Orbók). New York: Brentano's, 1924.

Sancho Panza [1923] (Adaptation of *Sancho Panza Királysága* by Melchior Lengyel). Typescript dated April 1921, in offices of Brandt and Brandt Dramatic Dept., Inc., New York.

Bewitched [1924] (With Edward B. Sheldon). Typescript in Theatre Collection, Houghton Library, Harvard [1922].

Three Flights Up (four short stories). New York: Scribner's, 1924. Contains "The God They Left Behind Them," "Mrs. Vietch: A Segment of Biography," "Transatlantic," and "A Likeness of Elizabeth," first appearance in *McCall's*, 52 (November, 1924).

163

They Knew What They Wanted [1924]. New York: Doubleday, Page & Co., 1925.

"Such Women as Ellen Steele" (short story), *Scribner's Magazine*, 77 (January, 1925), pp. 64–74.

Michael Auclair [1925] (Translation of *Michel Auclair* by Charles Vildrac). In Garrett H. Leverton (ed.), *Plays for College Theatre*. New York, 1932.

Lexington [1925]. Lexington, Massachusetts: Lexington Historical Society, 1924.

Lucky Sam McCarver [1925]. New York: Charles Scribner's Sons, 1926. In Montrose J. Moses (ed.), *Representative American Dramas*. Boston: Little, Brown & Co., 1941.

The Last Night of Don Juan [1925] (Translation of *Le Dernière nuit de Don Juan* by Edmond Rostand). Howard Collection, Berkeley [1925].

Morals [1925] (An arrangement of Ludwig Thoma's *Morality*, translated and adapted by Charles Recht in 1905). Typescript. Theatre Collection, New York Public Library, 1925.

Ned McCobb's Daughter [1926]. New York: Charles Scribner's Sons, 1926. In Fred B. Millet and Gerald Bentley (eds.), *The Play's the Thing*. New York: Appleton-Century Co., 1936.

The Silver Cord [1926]. New York: Charles Scribner's Sons, 1927.

Salvation [1928] (with Charles MacArthur). Prompt Copy, Theatre Collection, New York Public Library, 1928.

Olympia [1928] (Translation of play by Ferenc Molnar). New York: Brentano's, 1928.

"The Homesick Ladies" (short story). *Scribner's Magazine*, 85 (April,, 1929), pp. 379–94. In Blanche Colton Williams (ed.), *O. Henry Memorial Award Prize Stories of 1929*. New York: Doubleday, Doran & Co., 1930, pp. 29–51.

Half Gods [1929]. New York: Charles Scribner's Sons, 1930.

Lute Song [1930] (Adaptation with Will Irwin of *Pi-Pa-Ki* by Kao-Tong-Kia). Chicago: Dramatic Publishing Co., 1955.

One, Two, Three [1930] (Translation of one-act by Ferenc Molnar, *One, Two, Three, President!*). New York: Samuel French, 1952.

Marseilles [1930] (Translation of *Marius* by Parcel Pagnol). Prompt Copy, Theatre Collection, New York Public Library, 1930.

The Late Christopher Bean [1932] (Adaptation of *Prenez garde à la peinture* by René Fauchois). New York: Samuel French, 1933.

Alien Corn [1933]. New York: Charles Scribner's Sons, 1933.

Dodsworth [1934] (Adaptation of novel by Sinclair Lewis). New

York: Harcourt Brace & Co., 1934. In H. Hatcher (ed.), *Modern American Dramas*. New York: Harcourt Brace & Co., 1941.

Yellow Jack [1934] (with Paul de Kruif). New York: Harcourt Brace & Co., 1934.

Gather Ye Rosebuds [1934] (with Robert Littell). Copyright 1934 as "Bird of our Fathers." Typescript, Howard Collection, Berkeley.

Ode to Liberty [1934] (Adapted from *Liberté Provisoire* by Marcel Duran). Typescript in Theatre Collection, New York Public Library.

Paths of Glory [1935] (Adaptation of novel by Humphrey Cobb). New York: Samuel French, 1935.

The Ghost of Yankee Doodle [1937]. New York: Charles Scribner's Sons, 1938.

Madam, Will You Walk? [1953]. New York: Dramatists Play Service, 1955. In *Theatre Arts*, 41 (February, 1957).

2. *Films (screenplays by Howard unless otherwise indicated).*

Arrowsmith, 1931. (Based on the Sinclair Lewis novel.) Samuel Goldwyn, United Artists; with Helen Hayes, Ronald Colman, and Richard Bennett.

Brothers Karamazov, n.d. Not produced. (Based on the Dostoevsky novel.) Samuel Goldwyn.

Bull Dog Drummond, 1929. (Based on H. C. McNeile stories.) Sidney Howard, dialogue; screenplay by Wallace Smith. Samuel Goldwyn; with Joan Bennett and Ronald Colman.

Condemned, 1929. (Based on the Mrs. Blair Niles Novel.) Samuel Goldwyn; with Ann Harding, Ronald Colman, and Louis Wolheim.

Dodsworth, 1936. (Based on the Sinclair Lewis novel.) Samuel Goldwyn, United Artists; with Walter Huston and Ruth Chatterton.

Gone With the Wind, 1939. David Selznick, MGM; with Clark Gable and Vivien Leigh. Howard Collection, Berkeley.

The Greeks Had a Word For Them, 1932 (Based on the Zoë Akins play, *The Greeks Had a Word For It*). Samuel Goldwyn, United Artists; with Madge Evans, Joan Blondell, and Ina Claire.

Half Gods: filmed as *Free Love*, 1930. Screenplay by Winifred Dunn and Edwin Knopf. Universal; with Conrad Nagel and Ilka Chase.

It Can't Happen Here [1936]. (Based on the Sinclair Lewis novel.) Not produced. MGM.

The Late Christopher Bean: filmed as *Christopher Bean*, 1933.

Screenplay by Sylvia Thalberg and L. E. Johnson, MGM; with Marie Dressler, Lionel Barrymore, and Beulah Bondi.

The Light That Failed. (Based on the Rudyard Kipling novel.) Screenplay completed 1935, but another script by Robert Carson used for 1939 film. Howard Collection, Berkeley.

Lucky Sam Carver: filmed as *We're All Gamblers*, 1927. Screenplay by Hope Loring, with Thomas Meighan and Marietta Millner.

Ned McCobb's Daughter: filmed as *Ned McCobb's Daughter*, 1929. Screenplay by Beulah Marie Dix. Silent film, with Irene Rich, Robert Armstrong, and Carole Lombard.

Ode to Liberty: filmed as *He Stayed for Breakfast*, 1940. Screenplay by P. J. Wolfson, Michael Fessier, and Ernest Vajda, Columbia; with Loretta Young, Melvyn Douglas, and Alan Marshall.

Olympia: filmed twice, writers unknown, as *His Glorious Night*, 1929, MGM; and as *A Breath of Scandal*, 1960, Paramount.

One Heavenly Night, 1931. (Based on a Louis Bromfield story.) Samuel Goldwyn; with Evelyn Laye, John Boles, and Leon Errol.

One, Two, Three: filmed as *One, Two, Three*, 1961. Screenplay by Billy Wilder and I. A. L. Diamond. With James Cagney, Arlene Francis, Horst Burcholz, and Pamela Tiffin.

Paths of Glory: filmed as *Paths of Glory*, 1957. Writer unknown. Stanley Kubrick, United Artists; with Kirk Douglas, Ralph Meeker, and Adolphe Menjou.

Raffles: filmed twice. (Based on E. W. Hornung stories.) 1930: Samuel Goldwyn; with Ronald Colman and Kay Francis, 1940: screenplay by Howard and John Van Druten, with David Niven and Olivia de Haviland.

The Silver Cord: filmed as *The Silver Cord*, 1933. Screenplay by Jane Murfin. RKO; with Irene Dunne, Joel McCrea, Frances Dee and Laura Hope Crews.

They Knew What They Wanted: filmed three times. 1928: silent film as *The Secret Hour*. Screenplay by Rowland McKee, Paramount; with Pola Negri and Jean Hersholt. 1930: as *A Lady to Love*, MGM; with Edward G. Robinson, Vilma Banky, and Robert Ames. 1940: as *They Knew What They Wanted*. Screenplay by Robert Ardrey, RKO; with Charles Laughton, Carole Lombard, and William Gargan.

Yellow Jack: filmed as *Yellow Jack*, 1938. Screenplay by Edward Chodorov, MGM; with Robert Montgomery, Lewis Stone, and Henry Hull.

3. *Journalism, Essays, Interviews, Letters (a chronological listing).*

"Baiting the Bolshevist" (journalism). *Collier's,* 65 (January 10, 1920), 15, 24, 26. Favors an objective view of Russian Americans.

"The Colyer Trial Opens" (journalism). *The Survey,* 44 (April 17, 1920), 105; "In Judge Anderson's Court," *The Survey,* 44 (May 1, 1920), 182–84; "Judge Anderson's Decision," *The Survey,* 44 (July 3, 1920), 489–90. Favors due process in deporting radical aliens.

"The Labor Spy" (journalism with Robert Dunn). *The New Republic,* 25 (February 16, 23, 1921); 26 (March 1, 9, 16, 23, 30, 1921). Reprinted as *The Labor Spy.* New York: Republic Publishing Co., 1924, with three-fourths additional material. On the organized subverting of labor unions.

"Flowers That Bloom in the Spring (A Bouquet of Young Writers)" (essay). *The Bookman,* 53 (April, 1921), 116–22. Satirical essay on young poets and their art.

"Three Soldiers" by John Dos Passos (review). New York *Times* (October 19, 1921), sec. vii, p. 4.

"The Inside Story of Dope in This Country" (journalism). *Hearst's Internatonal,* 43 (February, March, April, May, June, 1923), 44 (July, 1923).

"Stock Swindlings: The Great Modern Shell Game" (journalism). *Hearst's International,* 44 (October, 1923), 18.

"Oil Crooks" (journalism). *Hearst's International,* 44 (November, 1923), 31.

"Our Professional Patriots" (journalism with John Hearley. *The New Republic* (August 20, September 3, 10, 17, 24, 1924). Enlarged to *Professional Patriots,* ed. Norman Hapgood. New York: Albert and Charles Boni, 1927. Free speech endangered by postwar patriotism.

"Where the New Guild Play Was Found by its Author" (interview). New York *World* (December 7, 1924). *They Knew What They Wanted.*

"Sidney Howard on the O'Neill Play" (review), New York *Times* (December 14, 1924), sec. viii, p. 4. On *Desire Under the Elms.*

Preface to *They Knew What They Wanted* (essay). New York: Doubleday, Page & Co., 1925. The source is Tristran and Yseult.

"Two Pulitzer Prize Winners Tell How It Feels and How They Did It" (interview by Flora Merrill). New York *World* (May 3, 1925). *They Knew What They Wanted.*

"Fruit Ranch Foreman is Pattern" (interview). New York *Post* (May 16, 1925). *They Knew What They Wanted.*

"Poet, Dramatist and Art Dealer" (interview). *Provincetown Theatre Playbill*, Season 1924–1925, n. 5, pp. 1–2, 4. For the *Michel Auclair* production.

"He Knew What He Wanted" (interview by Willis Coleman). *Theatre Magazine*, 42 (September, 1925), pp. 10, 52. Howard prefers people over philosophic ideas.

Preface to *Lucky Sam McCarver* (essay). New York: Charles Scribner's Sons, 1926, pp. vii–xxvii. The brave intentions of a failure. Plays are for actors.

"Lo the Poor Managers" (essay). *Vanity Fair*, 26 (May, 1926), 49. The aims of the Dramatists Guild.

"Escape" in "After Dullness, What?" (essay). *Survey*, 57 (November 1, 1926), 182. One of a group of articles by various authors on the theme, "After Dullness, What?"

"The American Lingo" (essay). New York *Sun* (December 4, 1926).

"The Prodigious Yankee" (interview). New York *Post* (December 11, 1926).

"Sidney Howard Speaking" (speech). New York *Times* (March 20, 1927), sec. xiii, p. 4. Excerpts from commencement address at the American Academy of Dramatic Arts. The writer is dependent on the actor.

Preface to *Olympia* (essay). (Translation of play by Ferenc Molnar.) New York: Brentano's, 1928. Same subject as "Shedding Light on the Labor of Translation," New York *Herald-Tribune* (October 14, 1928).

"Views of the Motion Picture Industry" (essay). New York *Times* (December 1, 1929), sec. x, p. 8. "At best, Hollywood is not a place to stay in overlong."

"Hollywood on the Slide" (essay). *The New Republic*, 72 (November 9, 1932), 350–53. Hollywood shies away from the realistic and disturbing.

"George Pierce Baker of Harvard and Yale" (essay). New York *Times* (February 5, 1933), sec. ix, p. 3. On the occasion of Prof. Baker's retirement. "He taught his students truth."

In Rehearsal (interview). New York *Times* (February 19, 1933), sec. ix, pp. 3, 6. Rehearsals are Howard's workshops; he readily cuts.

"A Postscript on Dramatization" (essay). *Dodsworth* (adaptation of novel by Sinclair Lewis). New York: Harcourt Brace & Co., 1934. The book contains a companion article by Lewis on dramatizing the novel.

Preface to *Yellow Jack* (essay). New York: Harcourt Brace & Co.,

1934. Also, New York *Times* (March 11, 1934), sec. x, p. 1. The historic basis: "A realistic historical play in seven realistic scenes."

"A Foreword for All College Theatres and for All Amateurs of Military Age" (essay). *Paths of Glory* (adaptation of novel by Humphrey Cobb). New York: Samuel French, 1935. Excellent major comments on dramatizing an "indictment of war." Advice for college production around a war memorial.

"The Playwright Tells All" (interview). *Stage,* 12 (February, 1935), 21–22. Excellent sketches by O. Soglow. Lighthearted general comments on Broadway: "I have written my own last play again and again."

Commencement Address to the American Academy of Dramatic Arts (speech). New York *Times* (March 29, 1936), sec. ix, p. 1. Legitimate stage actors superior to Hollywood stars.

The Ghost of Yankee Doodle (essay), New York *Times* (November 21, 1937), sec. xi, p. 1. Major comments on making "dramatic a scene of purely intellectual discussion."

Interview by George Brinton Beal. Boston *Post* (July 11, 1937). Beal, classmate in Baker's 47 Workshop at Harvard.

"Sidney Howard Loves Nearly Everything Except Things Like Social Messages" (interview by Michael Mok). New York *Post* (August 16, 1939). On *Madam, Will You Walk?*

"Sidney Howard: In His Letters" (letters). *Intimate Portraits* by Barrett H. Clark, Port Washington, New York: Kennikat Press [1951], rpt. 1970, pp. 181–226. Also, "Letters from Sidney Howard" by Barrett H. Clark, *Theatre Arts* (April, 1941), pp. 270–86, a selection of the above but with some editing. The only published letters of Howard, assembled by a very close friend.

SECONDARY SOURCES

ADAMS, HENRY H. "Sidney Howard: A Critical Study." Unpublished Manuscript dated "New York City, March 19, 1940." Howard Collection, Berkeley. Good detailed account of play criticisms. Comparisons of adaptations to original works.

ATKINSON, BROOKS. *Broadway.* London: Cassell, 1970. Consistent, perceptive views. Sees Howard as vigorous man of his times.

————— and Albert Hirschfield. *The Lively Years: 1920–1973.* New York: Associated Press, 1973. Essays and sketches of selected plays.

BACON, LEONARD. *The Saturday Review of Literature* (September

2, 1939), p. 8. Howard obituary by a close friend. Howard was immensely curious about everything, never bored or boring. He had a "sympathetic interest that played like fire over everything human."

BEHLMER, RUDY (ed.). *Memo from David O. Selznick*. New York: The Viking Press, 1972. The day-to-day memos, letters, and telegrams on the *GWTW* production.

BEHRMAN, S. N. *People in a Diary*. Boston: Little and Brown, 1972. Valuable personal recollections of the founding of the Playwrights' Company and the production of *Madam, Will You Walk?*

BROWN, JOHN MASON. "The Gamut of Style," *Theatre Arts Monthly*, 11 (February, 1927), 96–99. On *Ned McCobb's Daughter*: rises above melodrama by the "pungency and honesty" of the characters.

————. *Upstage: The American Theatre in Performance*. New York: W. W. Norton, 1930. Excellent appraisals of Howard's work in the 1920's.

————. *The Worlds of Robert Sherwood*. New York: Harper and Row, 1962. Knowledgeable account of the Playwrights' Company.

CLARK, BARRETT H. *An Hour of American Drama*. Philadelphia: J. B. Lippincott Co., 1930, pp. 77, 88. Sees Howard's technique as secondary to the subject matter.

————. "His Voice Was American," *Theatre Arts* (April, 1949), p. 30. Personal and critical appraisals by a very close family friend.

————. *Intimate Portraits*. Port Washington, New York: Kennikat Press, 1951, rpt. 1970, pp. 181–226. (One of six portraits which includes Maxim Gorky, John Galsworthy, Edward Sheldon, George Moore, and Carl Clinton.) Very valuable introductions to a selection of Howard letters by a close, intimate friend.

CLURMAN, HAROLD. *The Fervent Years*. London: Dennis Hobson, 1946. On *Yellow Jack* as a prospective production for the Group Theatre.

COSTY, JAMES O. "A Critical Evaluation of the Selected Plays of Sidney Howard." Ph.D. Dissertation, Denver, 1955. A useful review of the criticism of the major plays.

CRAVEN, BERNARD H. "Sidney Howard, The Man and His Plays." M.A. Thesis, University of California at Los Angeles, 1950. Written under the direction of Kenneth MacGowan, director of the Provincetown Players in the 1920's and associate of Sidney Howard.

DE KRUIF, PAUL. "Backstage with 'Yellow Jack,'" *Stage* (June, 1938), pp. 28–29. An account of the use of the author's *Microbe Hunters* as the source for the play.

FADIMAN, CLIFTON. "Bypaths of Glory," *Stage*, 13 (November, 1935), pp. 46–47. Excellent account of the difficulties in adapting the best-selling Cobb novel into Howard's *Paths of Glory*.

HORNBLOW, ARTHUR. *Theatre Magazine*, 41 (February, 1925), p. 19; and 42 (July, 1925), p. 7. A guarded appraisal of *They Knew What They Wanted*; reservations about the moral appropriateness of the Pulitzer Prize winner.

HOUSMAN, A. L. "The Working Methods of Sidney Howard," Ph.D. Dissertation, University of Iowa, 1956. Concentrates on technical as well as creative challenges in play productions. Excerpts in "Sidney Howard and Production," *Educational Theatre Journal (ETJ)*, 11 (March, 1959), pp. 13–16.

HOWARD, BRONSON. *The Autobiography of a Play.* New York: Dramatic Museum of Columbia University, 1914. Howard's famous address at Harvard, 1886, giving his "laws of dramatic construction."

HUGHES, GLENN. *A History of the American Theatre, 1700–1950.* London: Samuel French, 1951, pp. 396, 397. Compares Howard favorably with O'Neill as an innovator in the use of strong realistic characters.

ISAACS, EDITH. "Sidney Howard," *Theatre Arts*, 23 (October, 1939), 723. Obituary article by the editor of the publication.

KINNE, WISNER PAYNE. *George Pierce Baker and the American Theatre.* Cambridge: The Harvard Press, 1954. An excellent biography of the founder of the 47 Workshop, inspiration for numerous playwrights.

KRUTCH, JOSEPH WOOD. *The Nation*, 136 (March 15, 1933), 299. Review of *Alien Corn*: How Convincing is the frustrated artist?

———. *American Drama Since 1918.* London: Thames & Hudson, 1957, pp. 26–72. Good discussion of three new realists (Maxwell Anderson, Sidney Howard, and George Kelly). Provocative analyses of Howard's major plays. A major work of criticism in placing Howard among his contemporaries.

———. "Sidney Howard, Storyteller," *Theatre Arts*, 41 (February, 1957), pp. 31–32, 91–92. Illustrated with good behind-the-scenes pictures of the *Alien Corn* and *Dodsworth* productions. Howard was very intelligent but the "least intellectual" of his group.

LAMBERT, GAVIN. *GWTW: The Making of "Gone With the Wind."* Boston: Atlantic-Little, Brown, 1973. A well written account by an English film critic and novelist, who seems to have personally known many of the principals.

LEWIS, SINCLAIR. "The Art of Dramatization," *Dodsworth* (the play, adapted by Sidney Howard). New York: Harcourt, Brace & Co., 1934. A very revealing account of the problems that Lewis and Howard meet in dramatizing the novel. Published with a companion article by Howard.

LEWISOHN, LUDWIG. "Drama: Homespun and Brocade," *The Nation*, 113 (September 21, 1921), 324, 325. Review of *Swords*: Too literary; the work of a college senior. Better to write of "a coal miner's cottage in the Virginia mountains."

MESERVE, WALTER J. "Sidney Howard and the Social Drama of the Twenties," *Modern Drama*, 6 (December, 1963), 256–66. A major critical essay placing Howard historically with the social dramatists. Independent in spirit, Howard is not the experimenter other are. Nevertheless, in the decade of O'Neill, Sidney Howard is the "first major writer of social drama."

QUINN, ARTHUR HOBSON. *A History of the American Drama From the Civil War to the Present Day*. London: Sir Isaac Pitman & Sons, 1937. A major reference work. Excellent history, bibliography, and play summaries.

RICE, ELMER. *Minority Report: An Autobiography*. New York: Simon and Schuster, 1963. Personal recollections by another member of the Playwrights' Company.

SCHORER, MARK. *Sinclair Lewis*. New York: McGraw-Hill Book Co., 1961. Revealing, amusing anecdotes on the Lewis-Howard "collaborations."

SCOTT, CHARLES. "Sidney Howard," Ph.D. Dissertation, Yale, 1963. Informative introduction to the man and his works. Conversations with Howard's widow.

STUTZMAN, GERTRUDE. "Sidney Howard, Playwright and Personality," M.A. Thesis, University of Washington, 1947. To quote George Jean Nathan: "Adequate if not good." Despite the weak organization and writing, the copious facts of production are useful. Heavy reliance on Burns Mantle volumes.

TEMPLE, JOHN. "Sidney Howard: A Biographical Sketch and Bibliography," *Asides*, #2 (Stanford University Dramatists Alliance), 1941. A stenciled bound publication. Some "intimacy" in the biography; has interviewed relatives and friends. A valuable source.

THOMAS, BOB. *Selznick*. New York: Doubleday & Co., Inc., 1970.

Breezy, "pop" account of a celebrity. Useful film credits, anecdotes about *GWTW*.

THOMPSON, DOROTHY. "On the Record." New York *Herald-Tribune* (August 28, 1939), p. 14. Obituary column by a personal friend. Compassionate references to the irony of an idealist's death by a machine. "You saw in humans folly rather than sin."

Time. 23 (March 19, 1934), pp. 36–37. Good, complimentary sketch of career.

————. 23 (June 7, 1937). Cover article; reviews career.

TOOHEY, JOHN L. *A History of the Pulitzer Prize Plays.* New York: The Citadel Press, 1967, pp. 40–46. Good pictures and a selection of drama reviews for each play.

WHARTON, JOHN F. *Life Among the Playwrights: Being Mostly the Story of the Playwrights' Producing Company.* New York: New York *Times* Book Co., 1974. Engaging accounts of lawyer Wharton's involvement with New York theater. Well illustrated.

WILLIAMS, EMLYN. "The Late Christopher Bean," *Famous Plays of 1933.* London: Victor Gollancz Ltd., 1933. The English version based on the same René Fauchois original.

YOUNG, STARK. *Immortal Shadows.* New York: Scribner's, 1948. Collected Broadway reviews, written with style and conviction. On *The Silver Cord*: needs a "deeper texture of life."

Index

(The works of Howard are listed under his name)

Abe Lincoln in Illinois (Sherwood), 33
Academy Award, 30, 33, 126
All My Sons (Miller), 117
American Academy of Dramatic Arts, 140
American Defense Society, 24
American Legion, 24, 143
Ames, Winthrop, 28
Anderson, John, Judge, 23
Anderson, Maxwell, 33, 122
Arrowsmith (Lewis), 30
Association of American Dramatists, 28
Atkinson, Brooks, 97, 142
Austen, Jane, 21

Bacon, Leonard, 20
Baker, George Pierce, 20, 25, 147n2
Balderston, John, 129
Balzac, Honoré, 22
Barry, Philip, 127
Barrymore, Ethel, 114, 141
Beach, Lewis, 20
Beaumont, Francis, 21
Behrman, S. N., 20, 33, 118
Benet, Stephen Vincent, 26
Beyond the Horizon (O'Neill), 71
Braithwaite, Lillian, 77
Breen, Joseph, 130
Broun, Heywood, 27
Brown, John Mason, 71, 141
Brunetiere, Ferdinand, 22

Cabell, James Branch, 22, 24
Carson, Robert, 126
Chapman, John, 87

Clark, Barrett, 19, 22, 25, 29, 31, 56, 81, 97, 109, 118, 124, 125, 144
Clurman, Harold, 123
Cobb, Humphrey, 32, 110
Cohan, George M., 123
Colliers, 23
Colman, Ronald, 29, 126
Colyer, William, 23
Cornell, Katherine, 31, 95, 97, 110, 141
Crews, Laura Hope, 77, 141
Cukor, George, 129

"Daisy Miller" (James), 133
Daly, Augustin, 141
Damrosch, Walter, 30, 92
d'Annunzio, Gabrielle, 22
Dante, 54
de Kruif, Paul, 105, 142
Del Sarto, Andrea, 20
Desire Under the Elms (O'Neill), 26, 49, 57, 58, 137
Dodsworth (Lewis), 31
Dramatist Guild, 31
Dreiser, Theodore, 40, 43, 54, 133
Drinkwater, John, 25
Dunn, Robert, 23

Edwards, Jonathan, 45, 58
Emerson, Ralph Waldo, 80-81
Enemies (Gorky), 117

Fadiman, Clifton, 113
Fauchois, René, 31
Faust (Goethe), 118, 123-24
Fedra (d'Annunzio), 22

Fitzgerald, F. Scott, 60, 65, 129, 134, 159n9
Fleming, Victor, 129
Fletcher, John, 21
Foster, Michael, 129
Foster, William Z., 143
Frankfurter, Felix, 24
Freud, Sigmund (Freudian theories), 71, 76, 79, 92
Frohman, Daniel, 141

Galsworthy, John, 20
Garrett, Oliver H. P., 129, 130
Germany, 144
Gillmore, Frank, 28
Gillmore, Margalo, 141
Goethe, 118
Gorky, Maxim, 117
Great Gatsby, The (Fitzgerald), 60, 65, 136

Hapgood, Norman, 24
Hardwicke, Cedric, 123
Hearley, John, 24
Hearst's International, 23, 24
Hecht, Ben, 127, 129, 130
Hornblow, Arthur, 57, 74, 126
Houseman, John, 87
Houston, Walter, 104
Howard, Bronson, 141
Howard, Clare ("Jennifer") (daughter), 30
Howard, Clare Jennes Eames (first wife), 25, 28-30, 77, 140, 141
Howard, Helen Louise Coe (mother), 19
Howard, John Lawrence (father), 19, 20
Howard, Leopoldine ("Polly") Blaine Damrosch (second wife), 30, 92, 122
Howard, Margaret (daughter), 30
Howard, Sidney (daughter), 30
Howard, Sidney Coe: ambulance corps, 21; ancestry, 19; combat pilot, 21, 22; censorship attacks, 27, 28; death, 34; early plays, 20, 21, 36; early youth, 19; education, 20; film writing, 130-32; Harvard, 20, 36; Hollywood, 29, 30, 33, *125-32*; honorary degree, 32; ideas for plays, 30, 34; journalist, 22-25; marriage failure, 28, 29, 78; modern women, 133-37; morality and drama, 137-38; playwriting secondary to acting, 139-40; theater spokesman, 31; Tyringham farm, 30, 34; University of California at Berkeley, 20

WORKS—DRAMA:
Alien Corn, 31, *92-98*, 126, 134, 137
Bewitched, 26, *37-38*, 98, 142
Casanova, 26
Cranbrook Masque, The, 21, 36
Dodsworth, *98-104*, 105, 135, 142, 144
Ghost of Yankee Doodle, The, 25, 32, *113-18*, 126, 134, 137, 144
Half Gods, 29, *78-82*, 92, 98, 105, 135
Late Christopher Bean, The, 31, 41, *87-92*, 134, 137
Lexington, 28, 36, 83
Lucky Sam McCarver, 28, *60-66*, 83, 135, 139
Lute Song, 28, *83-87*, 126, 134, 142
Madam, Will You Walk?, 32, *118-24*, 126, 134
Marseilles, 42
Michael Auclair, 38-39
Ned McCobb's Daughter, 28, *66-71*, 78, 135
Ode to Liberty, 142
Paths of Glory, 32, 35, *110-13*, 114, 142
Salvation, 134, 142
S.S. Tenacity, 25, *38-39*
Sancho Panza, 26
Silver Cord, The, 28, *71-78*, 92, 134, 137, 145
Sons of Spain, The, 20

Swords, 25, 37
They Knew What They Wanted, 26, 27, *49-59*, 66, 78, 83, 92, 134, 137, 138, 142, 145
Yellow Jack, *105-10*, 113

WORKS—ESSAYS:
"Foreword for All College Theatres and for All Amateurs of Military Age, A" (*Paths of Glory*), 110
Ghost of Yankee Doodle, The, 114
"Hollywood on the Slide," 132
"Postscript on Dramatization, A" (*Dodsworth*), 103-104
Preface to *Lucky Sam McCarver*, 64-65, 139-40
Preface to *Olympia*, 142
Preface to *They Knew What They Wanted*, 54
"Sidney Howard Speaking," 140
"Views of the Motion Picture Industry," 131

WORKS—FILMS:
Arrowsmith, 30, 126, 130, 131
Brothers Karamazov, 126
Bull Dog Drummond, 29, 126, 131
Condemned, 29, 126, 131
Dodsworth, 126, 131
Gone With the Wind, 33, 104, 126, *127-30*
It Can't Happen Here, 32, 126
Raffles, 29, 126
They Knew What They Wanted, 126
Yellow Jack, 32

WORKS—JOURNALISM:
"Baiting the Bolshevist," 23
"Colyer Trial Opens, The," 23
"Inside Story of Dope in This Country, The," 24
Labor Spy, The, 23, 27
"Oil Crooks," 24
Professional Patriots, 24
"Stock Swindlings: The Great Modern Shell Game," 24

WORKS—SHORT STORIES:
"God They Left Behind Them, The" (*Three Flights Up*), 45-46
"Homesick Ladies, The," 29, *47-48*
"Likeness of Elizabeth, A" (*Three Flights Up*), 41-42
"Mrs. Vietch: A Segment of Biography" (*Three Flights Up*), 43-44
"Stars in Their Courses, The," 22, *40*
"Such Women as Ellen Steele," 46-47
"Transatlantic" (*Three Flights Up*), 42-43

Howard, Walter (son), 30

Irwin, Will, 28, 83, 86
Isaacs, Edith, 118

James, Henry, 28, 41, 46, 133, 134
Jones, Robert Edmond, 87
Jonson, Ben, 20
Journey's End (Sherriff), 110

Kelly, George, 38
Kerr, Walter, 124
Kipling, Rudyard, 20, 126-27
Knickerbocker Holiday (Anderson), 33
Kronenberger, Louis, 87
Krutch, Joseph Wood, 59, 71, 92, 110, 135, 142
Kubrick, Stanley, 32

La Guardia, Fiorello, 24
Leigh, Vivien, 129
Lewis, Sinclair, 30, 98, 103, 126, 144
Lewisohn, Ludwig, 37
Light That Failed, The (Kipling), 126-27
Littell, Robert, 26
Lord, Pauline, 135, 141
Lyly, John, 21

MacArthur, Charles, 129, 142
McCarthy, Desmond, 77
Mc Duffie, Duncan (Jean), Mrs.
  (sister), 19, 29, 125
McGowan, Kenneth, 37
Mac Kaye, Percy, 36
Machiavelli, Niccolo, 22
Main Street (Lewis), 99
Martin, Mary, 87
Massey, Edward, 20
Mayer, Edwin Justin, 129
Microbe Hunters (de Kruif), 105
Mielziner, Jo, 98, 105, 113
Mitchell, Margaret, 34, 128, 129
Miller, Arthur, 117
Miller, Winston, 129
Molnar, Ferenc, 141-42

Nathan, George Jean, 56, 112, 118
National Civic Federation, 24
National Security League, 24
Nazimova, Alla, 22
New Republic, The, 23

O. Henry Memorial Award, 47
Olivier, Laurence, 129
O'Neill, Eugene, 27, 38, 43, 49, 56,
  57, 58, 71, 92, 109, 137, 139, 142

Passos, John Dos, 143
Phoenix Theater, 123
Pickford, Mary, 25
Playwrights' Company, 31-33, 122,
  150n43
Portrait of a Lady (James), 134
Pulitzer Prize, 27, 57, 137
Pygmalion (Shaw), 66

Reed, Walter, Dr., 105-106
Rice, Elmer, 33, 38, 92, 122, 139

Rivet in Grandfather's Neck, The
  (Cabell), 22

Saroyan, William, 124
Scott, Raymond, 87
Selznick, David O., 33, 127, 128,
  130
Shaw, George Bernard, 66, 118, 124
Sheldon, Edward, 26, 37, 38, 142
Sherwood, Robert, 33, 122
Sister Carrie (Dreiser), 133
Skinner, Richard Dana, 92
Stallings, Laurence, 27
Stevenson, Robert Louis, 46
Spinoza, Baruch, 22
Swerling, Jo, 129
Swope, Bayard, 27

Theatre Guild, 28, 33, 73
Thompson, Dorothy, 34
Tyringham, Mass., 30, 34, 118

Van Druten, John, 126, 129
Vildrac, Charles, 25, 57
Voltaire, 22

Wagner, Richard, 54
Webster, Margaret, 123
Wharton, John, 122
What Price Glory (Stallings), 27,
  110
White, William Allen, 24
Wilder, Thornton, 109, 139, 142
Will Hays Office, 27, 32, 126, 130
Williams, Emlyn, 91
Wilson, Edmund, 143
Wiscasset, Maine, 28
Woman's Suffrage, 133

Young, Stark, 77

Zola, Emile, 22